A Day in June

And what is so rare as a day in June?
    Then, if ever, come perfect days;
Then Heaven tries earth if it be in tune,
    And over it softly her warm ear lays;
Whether we look, or whether we listen,
We hear life murmur, or see it glisten;
Every clod feels a stir of might,
    An instinct within it that reaches and towers,
And, groping blindly above it for light,
    Climbs to a soul in grass and flowers;
The flush of life may well be seen
    Thrilling back over hills and valleys;
The cowslip startles in meadows green,
    The buttercup catches the sun in its chalice,
And there's never a leaf nor a blade too mean
    To be some happy creature's palace;
The little bird sits at his door in the sun,
    Atilt like a blossom among the leaves,
And lets his illumined being o'errun
    With the deluge of summer it receives;
His mate feels the eggs beneath her wings,
And the heart in her dumb breast flutters
        and sings;
He sings to the wide world, and she to her
        nest—
In the nice ear of Nature which song is the
        best?
                                —Lowell

The image you see above was the illustration from the June 1920, *Inspiration* newsletter that was published by the Woman's Institute of Domestic Arts and Sciences which inspired my book *Vintage Notions*. For a more modern look, I chose to update this edition with the cover artwork from the Summer 1925 issue of Woman's Institute *Inspiration* magazine.

Edited by GUSTAVE L. WEINSS

The *Wages* of Study

BY THE EDITOR

AS SUMMER "just budded from the bud of spring" beckons one and all to spend as much time as possible in the open, there comes to us a feeling of freedom that is hard to define. We see before us many pleasures and are ready to share in the delights that summer affords. In fact, we are anxious for the life that will help us fortify our health for the sterner seasons that are to come—the outdoor games, the excursions to the parks and other pleasure resorts, the trips to the mountains, lakes, and seashore. And we realize, too, that summer is not a season for upbuilding health alone. Indeed, those of us who are striving to better ourselves are not unmindful of the fact that summer with its many privileges also affords an opportunity for us to increase our knowledge, and in so doing earn the wages that earnest, systematic study is bound to pay us.

THE wages of study are manifold. Everywhere about us we can see the good results that come from study, as well as the bad effects caused by the lack of it. As we observe the progress made by nations and man, we learn that those whose achievements are greatest are those whose enlightenment, whose knowledge, is greatest. And in no other way can knowledge be gained than by study, by cultivating the mind. Indeed, to quote from Seneca, "Just as the soil, however rich it may be, cannot be productive without culture, so the mind without cultivation can never produce good fruit."

PERHAPS the first wage we receive from knowledge gained by study is aroused ambition. When we find out that study allows us to share in the secrets of the learned, when we come to know that we can do the things that others have done and are doing, we have stirred up in us the desire to advance. This statement has been proved time and again by Institute students who, when they realize that they can learn to do the very things they have always wanted to do, are eager to advance. So even if this payment for study were our only reward, it would mean much. But ambition aroused leads on to achievement.

STUDY makes us self-reliant, thus paying us more wages. As we gain in knowledge, we can picture ourselves released from a bondage that threatened to make our lives fruitless. We can see before us a definite path beset, perhaps, with obstacles, but we are sure we can overcome them and travel on and on. To realize that we possess the power to help ourselves and that we can increase our worth by study is to progress with science and art and civilization. Faith in ourselves means victories won, for in the assurance of strength there is strength. Knowing that you can progress, you will progress.

STUDY makes us charitable, makes us feel for those who need assistance. After we have come to know that we can develop our own powers, we realize that we can and should help others. Indeed, this is the height of many a person's ambition. No greater act can we perform than to stretch forth a helping hand to those who need assistance. No greater deed can we do than to make better and brighter the lives of others.

AND, as if the wages of study mentioned were not enough, there is still more in store for those who see the way and continue to develop to a higher degree the powers with which they are endowed, for study really pays wages in happiness and success. When ambition is aroused and self-reliance is assured, the acts that can be performed must in themselves create happiness. And when happiness results from achievement, success is assured, for success cannot be counted as genuine unless the element of happiness enters in.

SO, AS the summer season comes upon us, be not aimless about your studies. A real thirst for knowledge cannot be satiated by a haphazard attempt at study. As the constant dripping of water wears away the stone, so systematic, regular, conscientious study will enable you to progress, and in progressing receive for your efforts the wages that are your just due.

Vintage Notions Monthly   ©2016 Amy Barickman, LLC

The Achievement of *Unselfishness*

By MARY BROOKS PICKEN
Director of Instruction

FOR nearly five years I have carried in a note book the one word *achievement*. All that time I have wanted to be equal to writing about it, because it stands definitely for the thing accomplished and, in its proper sense, means something very great.

The word *achievement* first took root in my consciousness when I heard a talented and great-hearted man state, "Achievement is the parent of sincere desire." I turned that statement over many times before I conclusively agreed that it is entirely true. My trend of thinking had been that we must first desire a thing before we would even set about to achieve it, but we can disprove that by the most elementary reasoning. For instance, with the first evidence of individuality in a child comes an effort for achievement. A step is accomplished and immediately the desire is created to try another; then two and three follow until the legs are strong enough to carry the body in motion.

All through life, as achievements are realized, desire is stimulated, and those who travel farthest are those who realize that great things are not accomplished by idle dreams or selfish motives, but by high appreciation, earnest effort, and patient and applicable study.

TO ASSOCIATE the word *achievement* with unselfishness seems the right thing, because real achievements, those which are permanent and lasting, must have their conception in unselfishness. Artist and teacher, philanthropist and minister, all must evidence extreme unselfishness to achieve heights in service.

But the highest achievements are reached by our mothers, for from them is exacted the greatest unselfishness and for them comes the greatest reward. Not long ago we were talking about this, and some one said, "Well, I've never been able to see where a mother had so much glory—always seems to me like a lot of sacrifice and hard work." Then it seemed the entire group arose in retaliation of this statement. Thinking machines were turned round and

light focused upon all the mothers we knew, and with every real mother we found a happy heart, perhaps traces of much suffering and unhappiness, but a soul made rich and hands made tender through that very service.

MEASURING achievements by individual standards or mile posts seems almost a shameful thing to do, and espe-

---

The Error of Selfishness

Imagine a rose that would say to itself: "I cannot afford to give away all my beauty and sweetness; I must keep it for myself. I will roll up my petals and withhold my fragrance."

But, behold, the moment the rose tries to store up its colors and treasures of fragrance, to withhold them from others, they vanish. The colors and fragrance do not exist in the unopened bud. It is only when the rose begins to open itself, to give out its sweetness, its life, to others that its beauty and fragrance are developed.

So human selfishness defeats its own ends. He who refuses to give himself for others, who closes the petals of his charity and withholds the fragrance of his sympathy and love, finds that he loses the very thing he tries to keep. The springs of his manhood dry up. His finer nature becomes atrophied. He grows deaf to the cries of help from his fellow men. Tears that never are shed for others' woes sour to stinging acids in his own heart.

Refuse to open your purse, and soon you cannot open your sympathy. Refuse to give, and soon you will cease to enjoy that which you have. Refuse to love, and you lose the power to love and be loved. Withhold your affections, and you become a moral paralytic. But the moment you open wider the door of your life and, like the rose, send out without stint your fragrance and beauty, you let the sunshine of life into your own soul.

---

cially if the measurements tend to a recognition of material success. Having things to do with and money to buy with is a satisfaction, but having some one to save for and plan with is real happiness.

A wonderful mother said to me recently, "Sometimes I can scarcely understand myself. Only a few years ago I had great ambitions to achieve success in business, and now I am perfectly content with just taking care of three babies, my husband, and our house." I realized, for I know her well, that she had not stopped being a success; rather, she had taken a bigger, broader road than that of business and had

become a Rose of Glory instead of a statuary trellis, as she might have been had business kept her interest.

IF EVERY mother could consider herself as a gardener in God's own garden, tending His roses, cultivating them, caring for them, keeping all the weeds and destructive things away, I am sure that being a mother would seem much more glorious. Often we get too close to real beauty to appreciate its magnificence. I wonder if that is why mothers sometimes grow tired and impatient—never getting far enough away from their own bit of garden to appreciate how truly wonderful it is.

Merchants take inventory at certain intervals, so as to know just what they possess and what they need. I have often wondered why it would not be a happy thing for our mother folk to take inventory to see just how precious their little live possessions need to make them even more precious.

Helping little folk to achieve speech, good manners, and unselfishness, putting into their hearts appreciation of life and all the good for which it stands, calls forth unselfishness in abundance, but results in the highest of achievements.

I KNOW a dear woman who has occasion to be very sad, but her cheerfulness is magnificent. She is so unselfish as to consider it actually wrong to allow any one to think of her grief. To see her is to appreciate thoroughly her sheer dexterity in concealment and to experience shame in having ever confessed a grievance. This woman possesses a true mother's greatest charm—unselfishness. To be in her presence is to appreciate the strength of her character and to love her for the happiness she manifests.

If I were so fortunate as to be an unselfish mother, a gardener in God's garden, I'd plant an abundance of happiness and I'd cultivate it with all my might, for I know for a certainty that seeds of unselfishness bring buds of happiness that blossom forth into glorious roses of Achievement.

Out in Life's garden, where sympathy grew,
God planted a soul—'twas the soul o' you.

Life's wonderful garden, Love, seeking, went through
Till he found a heart—'twas the heart o' you.

I have sought through life's garden of roses and rue
And I find one sweet blossom, all jeweled with dew—

Love, Sympathy, Faith—all unchanging and true—
Are the heart of my flower—dear Mother, 'tis you.

E. J. S.

Hats for *Growing Girls*

By MARY MAHON
Department of Millinery

IN ACCORDANCE with the trend of time, hats for growing girls and tiny tots are receiving just as much attention in the millinery centers as are those for growns-ups. In fact, whole establishments are given over to the making of misses' hats, and clever designers a r e devoting their entire time and thought to this branch of millinery. The result is that many charming designs are being shown and enough variety produced to suit every fancy without resorting to eccentricities, which very often make the young girl look ridiculous.

MISSES' hats should be very plain when they are to be worn with every-day costumes, but for more ceremonious occasions they may be somewhat dressy. Like their mothers and grown-up sisters, young girls wear dresses of silk, linen, net, and the other popular fabrics introduced each season; consequently, their hats are developed along the same lines and shapes as those for older persons, except that a few youthful touches are usually added.

Flexible hats made of taffeta and having pointed crowns and others with taffeta crowns and embroidered batiste brims that roll off the face, as illustrated at the right, are charming for the festive occasion when a taffeta, Georgette, or net dress is worn. For wear with organdies and ginghams, the hat may be made entirely of the same material as the dress.

IF YOU wish a hat for your daughter that will be appropriate for all occasions, it is necessary that you give it considerable thought before buying or making it. With hats of this kind, as well as all other hats, the features and general type of the girl must be carefully studied, so that a becoming hat of the correct size and shape may be selected. Then, too, variety can be had, even though only one hat is permitted in a season, by means of two or more adjustable sets of trimming.

Of all the different shapes, and there are a great many from which to select, the flat or straw body hat and its "first cousin," the modified poke, receive the preference for the growing girl. The crown can be a medium-sized dome or bell shape, depending on the features of the wearer. The model shown in the center picture, which has a medium-sized straw body, can be made suitable for wear on different occasions with very little effort. For one trimming, a wreath of pretty field flowers that blend well with the girl's frocks are combined with wheat and grasses. This wreath may be attached to a band of grosgrain or velvet ribbon and then drawn around the crown so that it lies flat on the brim. The ribbon is finished with a two-loop and two-end bow, and a hook and eye is sewed underneath so that the wreath may be removed when desired. Such a trimming makes a very smart hat for wear with a dark-silk frock or with a wrap on cool days in early summer.

TO MAKE this hat wearable with dainty summer frocks of organdie or net, a strip of the material 1½ inches wider than the brim and 1½ yards long is picoted on the outer edge and across the straight ends for a finish, and then accordion plaited or just shirred in ruffle effect to fit around the crown and the shirring bound with tape. This may be fastened at the back of the hat by means of a hook and eye, and should be allowed to extend out over the edge of the brim about 1 inch. Another strip of the material about 7 or 8 inches wide and 1½ yards long, picoted on both edges and across the bias ends, is draped as a sash around the side crown and tied in a bow at the back, the front, or the right side, depending on where it is most becoming to the wearer. This trimming may be easily removed if it is fastened by means of a hook and eye underneath the bow. It is advisable to make the bow and sew it on, as it will remain fresher looking than if it has to be tied each time it is removed.

Such an adjustable trimming of self-material serves a twofold purpose. In the first place, it gives a summery, fabric effect, which is so much desired in hats just now, and if it is made of wash material, it can be laundered very readily, a point to which you should give your attention if you would be spared much anxiety when your little daughter's hat becomes soiled.

THIS particular feature is a decided asset in the Baby Belle hat. This hat is made out of a piece of batiste 13 inches wide and 30 inches long, joined in a circle, and divided into four equal parts, the seam being used for the direct back. On the top edge, beginning at the center back, about 1 inch from the edge, cut off a strip, graduating this strip out to nothing at each side, and on the bottom edge cut off a similar strip. This makes the material narrower at the back than in front.

Next, turn the bottom edge in about 2½ inches in front and graduate the turning to about 1¾ inches at the back. Machine-stitch this hem and make a casing ¼ inch wide for a shirring tape or an elastic, and hem-stitch one row of Val lace to the outer edge of the hem. As a finish for the top edge, make a ¾-inch hem and hem-stitch a row of the Val lace on the direct edge, which will leave room for a shirring tape or an elastic. Sew a row of beading around the head-size directly over the casing and one on the top edge, and run a band of pink faille No. 5 ribbon through the beading. Run a shirring tape or a narrow elastic through the casing at the head-size to fit the head, and then draw the ribbon up through the beading and make a small bow at the left side. Also, draw up the shirring tape in the top as tight as possible and draw up the ribbon and make a bow at the right side, having ends in streamer fashion.

THE Baby Jane hat is made over a little foundation poke frame, and the material used may be embroidered Georgette crêpe or batiste, finished on the edge of the brim with a tiny lace. For trimming, a row of tiny hand-made chiffon flowers and foliage is used across the front, and a bow of picot-edged ribbon is fastened at the back.

In each of these hats, you will note that simplicity is the keynote. However, this should not be carried to the extreme, for severely plain hats are not becoming to all children. For instance, the tot whose hair is short and thin will require a little softness near the face, and the ribbon used for trimming will necessarily have to be a little wider and softer than that used ordinarily. Sometimes a soft frill of lace sewed at the head-size is all that is necessary to make the hat becoming. However, for the tot whose hair is fluffy and curly, the simple, severe-line hats are more desirable.

Early-Teen Frocks

By ALWILDA FELLOWS
Department of Dressmaking

THAT difficult "in-between" age—how deeply it concerns the majority of mothers, not only in regard to the rapidly changing ideas and habits of the miss who no longer takes a noticeable interest in doll's clothes, but also in the matter of providing becoming dresses, hats, and wraps that will suit her fancy. Perhaps, as yet, she has not fully awakened to the possibilities of expression in clothes and is inclined to be very carefree and somewhat neglectful, or at least indifferent, concerning her appearance. On the other hand, she may be unduly self-conscious because of the number of inches that, with alarming rapidity, have been attaching themselves to her person, principally in adding length to her arms and legs.

When one's proportions keep showing such a tendency to become unusual, it *is* rather difficult to neglect them entirely the greater part of the time. However, there is one very excellent means of making one feel at ease—it applies to grown-ups, as well—and that is the satisfaction of feeling suitably and comfortably dressed. When the wearing of one's clothes proves a pleasure rather than an incentive for uncomfortable feelings, self-consciousness, to a very great extent, is bound to find itself a losing factor.

ONE of the very important considerations in the dressing of a girl in her early teens is the appearance of her figure. She should be taught how to stand correctly in order that her dresses, which are built on more womanly lines, may hang properly and appear to their best advantage. If her carriage is not good and her abdomen rather prominent, she should without hesitancy be provided with a corset waist, for careful molding of the figure should not be neglected at this time. The corset waist will in no way prove detrimental to her health if it is very pliable, of good make, and is carefully fitted so that it will not hold the figure really tight at any point.

So often proper attention is not given to skirt and sleeve lengths for the growing girl. Skirt lengths should be made to adhere reasonably to fashion's dictates, but never to the sacrifice of becomingness and modesty. No set rule should be followed any season for girls of a certain age, for the proportions of each must be studied and treated differently.

Sleeve lengths in girl's dresses do not go to the extremes shown in styles for women. The extremely short sleeve is shown only occasionally, and then in the sheerest and most elaborate dresses. As this style is a rather trying one, it should be absolutely shunned in designing for a girl having very long, slender arms, and elbow-length sleeves supplied to detract from unusual arm length.

For another type of girl, a sleeve reaching just below the elbow might prove more suitable. In any event, sleeve lengths should be made to display the arms to the best advantage and no prescribed length followed.

NOW some definite suggestions as to styles. These should be comparatively loose and generally on rather straight lines —always suggestive of youthfulness. Simplicity is a factor that should not be lost sight of, for intricacy of design or elaborate decoration does not fit in well with the spirit of youth.

The requirements of suitable styles do not bar out unusual features, as is evidenced in the design shown at the left of the group. This dress is similar to one shown in a prominent New York children's shop and has already proved its desirability. If intended only for warm-weather wear, the dress may be made of an unusual combination, taupe linen or chambray for the blouse and taupe and green plaid gingham for the skirt. Stitching and a patent-leather belt in green will provide all the trimming necessary. If desired, the light-colored vestee may be omitted and the blouse itself finished with a round or an oval neck line.

Very many small plaits in the skirt would make it difficult to launder; therefore, if wash materials are chosen for the dress, the skirt should be merely gathered or laid in rather wide box plaits.

A silk or a wool overblouse of dark color worn with a steam-plaited plaid skirt is a variation of this style. The model would prove an excellent one for school wear and might be made during leisure time in the summer in anticipation of fall needs.

THE Royal design illustrated in the center of the group is particularly desirable for warm days. A sheer, pretty frock can do a great deal toward helping one forget the weather; and when sheer, pretty frocks are mentioned this season, one naturally thinks of dotted Swiss or organdie.

In choosing Swiss, selection may be made from an assortment of dots of various colors—pink, red, yellow, pale blue, green, etc. The trimming may be of white ruffles picoted in a color to match the dots.

A simple little dress such as this requires no special pattern. The blouse may be cut from a plain-kimono waist pattern extended to form the full peplum portion, or the peplum may be added as an extra section. The skirt may be of straight lengths of material banded with a strip of self-material finished on each edge with ruffles. A girdle of picoted ribbon may loosely confine the blouse fulness at the waist line.

VARIED possibilities in regard to materials are suggested by the remaining design. Crêpe de Chine or very soft taffeta in a light or a dark shade may be chosen from the silk fabrics, or if a dress for more ordinary wear is desired, pongee in natural color with a vest and a collar of a becoming shade of organdie would be effective.

Fine linen or any soft, light-weight cotton fabric might be substituted for any of the materials mentioned. The design also affords possibilities for the use of embroidery flouncing. In the waist portion, this may be cut so that the finished edge forms the lower edge of the sleeve.

Although this is a Royal design, there is no pattern for it. However, with the use of a well-fitting plain kimono-waist pattern, no difficulty should be encountered in its development, for it is a simple style.

THE summer issue of *The Children's Costume Royal* devotes a number of pages to styles for the girl in her early teens. A great deal of emphasis is laid on flutings, plaited skirts, flounces or tiered effects, and scallops.

In some instances, scalloped effects are piped with contrasting color or ornamented with several rows of rather heavy stitching. When used on organdie dresses, scallops are sometimes finished with a picoted edge or made of two thicknesses of material and occasionally finely blanket-stitched. Other popular trimming for organdie dresses consists of sections of inserted plaitings, tucks, or fine lace and insertion.

A Lunch in the *Open*

By LAURA MacFARLANE
Editorial Department

IN JUNE, the month of "perfect days," the pleasure of a trip to the neighboring woods and hills can hardly be estimated. All during April and May we have been welcoming the birds back, watching the trees and flowers break into bud and blossom, finding each day and each week a little brighter and balmier, and gradually realizing that we are nearing the "high tide of the year," when "skies are clear and grass is growing." So when June comes, even though we are not ardent devotees of Nature, we grow impatient for a whole day or even a few hours off, that we may cast aside all toil and care and hie ourselves away to some favorite spot, there to experience the joy and sense of relief that come from the abandonment of all duties and close contact with Nature. In fact, "At such a season," says Henry Van Dyke, "it is hard to stay at home. The streets all seem to lead into the country and one longs to follow their leading."

IT IS not necessary that a long trip be taken each time nor that a great distance be covered. Right in your own neighborhood, within easy reach of your home, I am sure there are more pretty spots than you dream of; only a few journeys will be needed to make you wonder why you never before appreciated the beauties of your own region. So at your first opportunity, jump into your automobile for a spin to the woods, board the near-by local for the country, or cover the distance with a leisurely jaunt, and then revel in the joys and the beauties that there await you. Or occasionally, when you cannot spare time for such an excursion, emulate the custom followed in England, where, especially in the country districts, the whole family, together with a number of guests and friends from the neighborhood, enjoy many a meal on the lawn under the shady trees.

ONE of the finest parts of an outing of any sort is the lunch. Seldom does one have such an appetite as after a tramp in the open, and never does food taste so appetizing as when it is cooked over the open fire or eaten in the quiet of the woods. And how refreshing is the draft of clear cold water one dips from the little spring near the roadside. Indeed, the memories of such refreshment linger for many days and call us back again and again. May I help you to plan your lunch for the outing I am sure you are going to enjoy very soon?

The kind of lunch to take depends largely on the length of time you can spend in the woods and the sort of outing you decide to have. Some persons like to prepare the entire lunch at home, pack it in a good-sized basket, or hamper, and then, upon reaching the chosen spot, spread a cloth and set everything out within easy reach of all. This is an excellent plan, especially when one is traveling by automobile and wants to spend more time in the journey than in the preparation of the meal.

THERE is considerable variety in such lunches and still only those things should be taken that will carry well. Sandwiches are practically a necessity, and they may be made out of white, brown, or nut bread and merely spread with butter, or they may contain a filling of some sort, such as cheese, meat, jelly, lettuce, peanut butter, and fruit. Be sure to make them very dainty and to wrap them in waxed paper in order to keep them fresh and moist. If sandwiches are omitted, buttered rolls may take their place and then jam or marmalade will be found most appetizing.

In addition to sandwiches, your lunch may contain a favorite salad, garnished attractively in a salad dish or divided into individual portions and packed in sanitary cups; baked beans, particularly if a hearty dish is desired; deviled or merely hard-cooked eggs; olives, pickles, tomatoes, or cucumbers, in the way of a relish; home-made cake in loaf, layer, or small-cake form; seasonal fruit; and hot coffee or a cold drink, such as iced lemonade, fruit punch, or tea, prepared at home and carried in a thermos bottle.

BUT, probably, you and the members of your party are enough of woodsmen to prefer to build a fire in some sheltered spot along a little winding stream and cook your meal over this. If you can spend enough time on your excursion for such a lunch, I hope you won't forego the pleasure it will bring you, as it will not only excel the home-prepared lunch, but give you a much closer contact with Nature and thus make your outing a real treat. And the splendid thing about cooking of this sort is that every one can take a part in it and thus, besides lightening the task involved, work up such an appetite as only the savory food that is being prepared can satisfy. Such things as rolls, bacon, frankfurters, steak, pickles, olives, radishes, potato salad, coffee, cake, fruit, and marshmallows make a goodly list from which an excellent selection may be made.

WHILE you are gathering the wood for your fire, cut a number of long, rather thick branches and trim these at the small end so that they contain two sharp-pointed prongs. Fasten a frankfurter on the prongs, twist a piece of bacon over this, and hold over the fire until the bacon is crisp and the frankfurter well cooked. These thrust into a Vienna roll and seasoned with mustard will make a sandwich that cannot be equaled, for the bacon adds just the desired touch, it being, as Van Dyke says, "aromatic, appetizing, nourishing, a stimulant to the hunger which it appeases."

However, if you are fortunate enough to be able to arrange many picnics of this kind, I would suggest that on some of them you substitute tender steak for bacon and frankfurters. A long-handled toaster is a splendid utensil for broiling steak in this way, or a grate that is supported with legs and may be placed directly over the fire may be procured.

IF YOU have never experienced the delight of a cup of coffee made in the woods, plan a picnic some time soon, especially for this privilege. Probably you have a good-sized coffee pot that you can use for just such occasions, but this is not really necessary, as most delicious coffee can be made in an ordinary pail. Before you leave home, put into a small muslin bag 1 tablespoonful of coffee for each person to be served, and either sew this up or tie it securely. Then, when your fire is at its best, place the bag in a pail, cover it with as many cupfuls of cold water as there are persons in your party, and allow the water to boil for several minutes. Served with sugar and rich cream, such coffee cannot be excelled.

As you are preparing and enjoying these things, your fire will gradually die down, but while it still contains a few hot embers, toast your marshmallows. Thrust several of these on one of the long sharp-pointed sticks and hold them over the fire until they turn a delicate brown. They will provide a splendid ending to your woodland lunch.

Woman's Institute *Question-Box*

Maternity Styles

May I ask for help in planning a maternity dress? I would also appreciate having suggestions for its adjustment. B. Y.

The front and back views of a style that has been designed especially for maternity wear are illustrated on this page. If you observe carefully the various features of this style, it will help you in the selection of other designs.

No tissue-paper pattern for this model may be had, but Pictorial Review blouse design 8464, with a few changes, may be used in cutting the waist, and the skirt may be of straight lengths of material or cut with the aid of a gored-skirt pattern having fulness at the waist line.

The horizontal tucks in the skirt, which are placed considerably below the hip line, draw attention from the unusual size at this point. Likewise, the trimming bands, which are an extension of the collar, serve to accentuate lengthwise lines through the waist and hip portions.

To overcome the rather flat appearance generally evident at the back waist line, the panel is looped under. This panel also serves to conceal the adjustable ends of the waist, which are made to extend from the under-arm seam and are cut long enough to permit them to be let out as the waist measurement increases.

Soft drapery in the front of the waist has a tendency to detract from the appearance of flatness of the bust as compared with the hips.

Fulness in the skirt may be adjusted by an elastic at the waist line, or the skirt may be applied to a loose net waist lining, to which, also, should be attached the sleeves of the dress. In cutting the skirt, the precaution should be taken to allow for an extension above the waist line at the center front, this extension to be rounded to the side and the skirt let down at the center front, when necessary.

Pictorial Review dress style 8650 is a special maternity design. It has loose front and back waist panels and a gathered overskirt. The pattern might be used without change or made with a deep oval neck line, and a light colored vestee supplied.

For a house dress, Butterick design 9913 is excellent. This consists of a loose overblouse and a straight gathered skirt.

Accordion-Plaited Skirt

Will you please give instructions for making an accordion-plaited skirt? H. C.

Plaiting of this kind must be done on a machine especially constructed for this purpose. By inquiring, you will undoubtedly learn of a shop in your vicinity that makes a specialty of this work.

In order to prepare the skirt for plaiting, cut three skirt lengths of 36-inch material, or only two lengths if the material is 54 inches wide. Join all the seams but one; then turn and stitch the hem in position. After the skirt is plaited, join the remaining seam and make the placket on this seam. Run a gathering thread at the upper edge of the skirt; then secure this to an inside stay belt, taking care that any difference in the front, side, and back skirt lengths is adjusted from the waist line, for it is, of course, impossible to change the hem after the skirt is plaited.

Removing Perspiration Stains

Please suggest a method for removing perspiration stains from a silk dress. E. B.

I believe you will find this practically impossible if the dress is nonwashable. Even professional cleaners are, in most instances, unable to remove such stains, although a thorough cleaning of the garment sometimes makes the stains less noticeable.

In washable garments, fresh perspiration stains may be removed by applying corn starch on the wrong side of the material and brushing this out after the material has dried. If this method does not prove effective, the stains may be soaked in a solution formed of equal parts of alcohol and water and then rinsed thoroughly in clear, cold water.

Want to Get Acquainted?

The following Institute students desire to become acquainted with other Institute students residing in their localities:

Indiana ....O. S.
Boston, Mass..............................L. Mc.
Russell, Minn............................W. B. S.
Burlington, Vt...........................G. A. L.
East Cleveland, Ohio....................C. W. K.
San Rafael, Calif.......................H. M. C.
Camden, N. J............................J. A. R.
South Lawrence, Mass....................H. R.
Tomah, Wis..............................A. C. G.
Burlington, Vt..........................H. L. B.
Willow Ranch, Calif.....................C. V.

I should like to correspond with girls of my age, 22 years, taking the Dressmaking Course.
L. M. P.

I should like to correspond with Woman's Institute students residing anywhere except in South Dakota. M. S.

I should like to become acquainted with Woman's Institute Dressmaking students of 18 or 20 years of age. V. C.

I should like to become acquainted with other students of the Woman's Institute.
Mrs. Eva Goffe,
70 Gibbs Ave., Newport, R. I.

I should like to correspond with some girl, between fifteen and nineteen years of age, who is taking the Millinery Course and resides in the state of Massachusetts, or a girl from some small town near Hudson. Miss Mardel E. Blongy,
202 Essex Co., Westport, N. Y.

I should like to correspond with some other student about my own age—18 years. M. I.

I should like to become acquainted with students of the Dressmaking Courses who live on, or very near, the border line between Wisconsin and Illinois. G. S.

I should like to become acquainted with some student taking the Complete Dressmaking Course who is left-handed.
Mrs. James G. Storrs,
1003 Walnut Ave., Rocky Ford, Colo.

If other Woman's Institute students would like to get in touch with the inquiring students, we shall be glad to supply the addresses that are not given.

Making Extension Tuck

In making the extension tuck on the edge of a transparent hat, how should the material be cut and the tuck applied? J. R. S.

Maline is used chiefly in the construction of transparent hats, and it is bias as it is wrapped on the bolt. Therefore, when you cut a length of maline, as you do in making the extension tuck, you have a bias piece. If you desire to apply a 1-inch tuck to the edge of the brim, determine the length of your edge wire and cut a strip of maline this same length, plus about 5 inches, and 7 inches wide. Fold this in half, and then in half again so as to make four thicknesses. Apply this fold to the edge of the brim, drawing its outer edge with the fingers so as to flare it a trifle, and lap it about 1 inch at the back for a joining.

If you are making the hat of Georgette crêpe, it will be necessary to cut the material for the tuck on a true bias, and as the crêpe is extra wide, the one strip will be sufficient to fit around a large-sized brim. This material requires a seam in the back, which can be made straight by cutting off the bias corners and joining the ends by machine.

Making Picoted Edge

How should I proceed to make a picoted edge on organdie ruffles? Is this work very tedious? P. F.

The finish you have in mind is undoubtedly that obtained by machine work. Such an edge is formed by having the material hem-stitched on a machine especially constructed for this purpose and then cutting the hem-stitching in two.

Hem-stitching machines are very expensive, and because they are suitable for only one purpose they are hardly practicable for the home dressmaker. However, it is possible to have machine hem-stitching done at a very small cost per yard at sewing-machine agencies or shops that specialize in this work.

In preparing ruffle material for hem-stitching, space rows of basting twice the desired ruffle width apart, to serve as a guide for the machine operator.

Our Students' *Own Page*

Saved $75 on a Suit

I wish to take this opportunity to tell you how delighted I am with your Course. I made for myself a gray broadcloth suit, and the entire cost, including thread and buttons, was only $25. Suits with material not so good cost from $75 to $135 in the shops. Dresses that cost me $15 are $35 and $45.

Miss Hattie Thorp,
Floydada, Tex.

Big Saving on Winter Coat

I've really made a great number of things, aside from helping friends in the mysteries of buttonholes and plackets! However, the thing I am the most proud of is my winter coat. I made this of brown velour, lined it with all-wool taffeta, and it cost me only $23.60. This, of course, didn't include a real sealskin collar which I had. I felt quite entitled to smile my most superior smile when my friends "cussed" the high prices of winter clothes.

Miss Marie Weidenbomer,
Moore, Mont.

Saved $75 on One Dress

I am enjoying my work immensely, and feel that it has been a great help to me. I copied a $98 dress this fall for $22.50 and feel well dressed in it.

Mrs. Murray H. Davis,
406 Hathaway Ave., Houston, Tex.

Saved Half on Husband's Silk Shirt

I wish to tell you what I have done since sending in my last lesson on Tissue-Paper Patterns. I made my husband two shirts, one of percale and one of silk. The percale one was a duplicate of a $3 one and cost $1.13, and the silk one was a duplicate of a $16 one and cost, including pattern and thread, $7.29. Isn't that great? I have saved what I have put into my Course so far.

Mrs. Adelaide H. Hugland,
Mt. Pleasant, Pa.

Spent $1 for Millinery Since She Joined

I have spent just $1 for millinery since beginning my Course—that was for ½ yard of crêpe de Chine—and I made a stunning little close-fitting hat for motoring. I found my idea in INSPIRATION, which is a jewel in itself. Just yesterday I made my oldest daughter a hat, a prettier one than I ever bought, and made over a black-velvet one of hers for my little 4-year-old. For myself, I made a fur hat and retrimmed an old one, all from materials I had on hand. I cleaned and curled a feather I thought was past cleaning, and it looks like new.

Mrs. Bessie Gould,
60 4th St., S. E., Carrollton, Ohio

What I Saved by Making My Own Clothes

While women everywhere are feeling the effects of the greatly increased cost of clothing, Woman's Institute members are having two or three dresses and hats for what they once paid for one. And now that they are able to design and make their clothes especially to express their own individuality, many of them are having prettier and more becoming clothes.

This note of economy has been sounded so often in the letters we have been receiving that we have decided to make it the keynote of our students' page this month. Each of the letters we are quoting comes from a woman who but a few short months ago was laboring with the problem of the high cost of clothing about as helplessly as most women are today, for the woman who must depend on the shops or the dressmaker is indeed extremely helpless to cope with this problem. But how different it is when she, like these women whose letters we are quoting, is able to design and make her own clothes. Her only expense is for material, and very often even that expense can be saved by making use of some of the perfectly good material that practically every woman possesses in clothing that has outlived the style.

Baby's $15 Coat at No Expense Whatever

For baby Ruth, I made a little white-wool serge coat and bonnet out of a suit that I had, and I am sure that they could not be purchased for less than $15. All they cost me was the thread and lining. I also made a number of little dresses and undergarments for her. For myself, I made a black-satin dress and embroidered it in delft blue. It made a very charming dress.

Mrs. John Caswell,
Schenectady, N. Y.

Saved Cost of Course in One Season

I saved the cost of my Course last fall in making over coats for my four children, for the coats I had selected to buy them would have cost that amount, and when I made over four coats I was better pleased with them than I would have been with boughten ones. I am sure I have better material in them. I have done all my sewing for my children since starting my Course.

Mrs. C. L. Bambrick,
Brooks Station, Alta., Canada

Saved $19 on Baby's Coat

I made a corduroy cap and coat for baby, using a McCall pattern. I trimmed the cap and coat with narrow bands of beaver fur. It looks very good on the corduroy. Mr. Bishop thought I made a pretty good job of it. It cost me only $6, as I had the fur. We looked at one very similar to it in Philadelphia, and it was $25.

Mrs. Norman B. Bishop,
Chester, Pa.

Clothes Now Costing One-Half

It is a pity to think that every girl and young woman isn't able to learn the value of your Courses. My Course has really made me happy, for I know that I wouldn't be able to procure the clothes I make for myself for twice the amount they cost me. I hope in time every one will learn its value, as it seems to me they will.

Miss Sophie Dulchinos,
153 Gratton St., Chicopee Falls, Mass.

A Broadcloth Dress for $12

Though I have taken only a few lessons, I can't begin to tell what good they have done me. I have been able to save so much for my own clothes as well as my sisters. Just lately I made a suit for myself, on which I saved a great deal. Also, I made a broadcloth dress that cost me only $12. I know it would have cost me at least $40 at the store. I am proud of my dress and suit.

Miss Lillian Boesson,
Galt, Sacramento Co., Calif.

Two Suits With Not One Cent of Expense

I just wish I could tell you how much the few lessons I have taken have helped me. When our two boys started for school, I couldn't see how we were to buy them new suits at the price we have to pay for things now. Just then your lessons on Tissue-Paper Patterns came, so I sent and got a pattern, measured the boys, and cut both a suit from one pattern. Every one asks where I bought such nice suits. And, now, for the secret—they were both made from old clothes. If I could only make every one see how much help they could get from even four lessons.

Mrs. Alex McKay,
Eddy, Mont.

SPECIAL NOTICE: For full information regarding Courses in Sewing, Dressmaking, Tailoring, Millinery, and Foods and Cookery as taught by the Woman's Institute, address all requests to the

WOMAN'S INSTITUTE OF DOMESTIC ARTS AND SCIENCES, Inc.

DEPT. 21, SCRANTON, PA.

Fashion Service
— SUPPLEMENT —

Each Issue of *Vintage Notions Monthly* includes a *Fashion Service Supplement*. You will read about the fashion styles popular in the early twentieth century and receive a collectible fashion illustration to print and frame.

The students of the Woman's Institute would also receive a publication called *Fashion Service*. Where the *Inspiration* newsletter instructed them on all aspects of the domestic arts, not only sewing but also cooking, housekeeping, decorating, etc., *Fashion Service* was devoted entirely to giving current fashions with a key to their development.

Fashion Service prided itself on providing it's readers with reliable style information and the newest fashion forecasting. The publication wasn't just eye candy. The Institute stressed the importance of studying the fashions to benefit the sewer's understanding of dressmaking. To quote founder Mary Brooks Picken, "Once the principles of design...and of construction... are understood, beautiful garments will result. This publication comes to you as an aid to this desired goal. Read the text of every page and reason out the why of every illustration and description that your comprehension of designing and construction may be enlarged and your appreciation made more acute."

Today, these articles and illustrations give us a historically accurate view of what fashion really meant 100 years ago. Not only can we study these articles for an "of-the-time" style snapshot, but just as their students did, we can also learn to understand the principles of design and increase our sewing skills. In each issue, look for a collectible illustration in the back of the supplement!

Suit Variations

Model 6A.—Along with the vogue for knitted garments in which there is so much promise for spring, it is but natural that both wool and silk in jersey weaves should be brought into prominence.

No promise of the serviceability of jersey need be made this season, for this point is one that was established not long after the fabric was first introduced. But assurance that the new weaves are much firmer and much less liable to stretch out of shape than the jerseys we have had in the past, is the very inviting reason we are given for accepting them this season.

As if doubly to guard against stretching, many garments made of knitted silk are trimmed in such a manner with straps of self-material or with braid that this trimming serves to maintain the closeness of weave as well as the original shape of the garment.

One of the various ways in which trimming is used to provide stay pieces is shown in this model of heavy knitted silk in a version of tan that is called lark.

An effect as novel as it is attractive is produced by the application of henna and of black braid. The henna color edges the Tuxedo collar and lower edge of the sleeves, besides being used for the upper and the two outside bands on the sleeves and for the center front and back and upper bands on the skirt. The black braid extends along the center of the sleeves and at each side front and side back of the jacket and skirt, and forms the lower band on the skirt and the center one on the sleeves.

A garment of knitted silk, to be entirely satisfactory, must be cut on straight simple lines, as are the jacket and the skirt of this model. The sleeve is flared just a trifle.

Average material requirements for this style include 5 yards 36 to 40 inches wide, with 12 yards of black braid and 13 yards of henna braid for trimming, and 1¾ yards of the henna braid in a wider width for the belt.

A lining is really not essential, but one might be employed, if desired. An extremely soft satin should be used for this purpose, in order not to detract from the softness of the suit fabric. A light tan that harmonizes with the color of the suit would be a good selection. Provide about 2 yards of this material.

Model 6B.—Just why, for so many years, we considered tweed merely from the point of utility without a thought of the possibilities and of the real beauty that might be brought out in its development is a question that a lovely model such as this cannot help but raise in one's mind.

A rather deep but soft, pleasing shade of pink is the color of the tweed, and lavender, green, and blue in harmonizing tones are the colors used for the wide bands of worsted embroidery that decorate each front edge of the jacket.

An enlarged detail of the embroidery carried out in darning-stitches is shown at the right. Without this trimming the jacket would be very plain, for it is cut with only normal seam lines and a slight flare that repeats itself in the sleeves.

A jacket of this kind is especially well adapted for wear over a one-piece dress, as illustrated, the entire suit thus being a variation of the three-piece costume.

Shown at the upper left is a full view of the dress. The waist portion of this is of white Canton crêpe. This, also, is very simple as to cut, being a slip-over kimono model with bands of the tweed arranged as illustrated as the only trimming.

Provide, for the average figure, 3¼ yards of 54-inch fabric, 2 yards of lining, 1⅝ yards of 40-inch contrasting material for the upper portion of the dress, and 12 small skeins of yarn.

Model 6C.—As interesting as the colorful and glorified models of tweed have proved, they in no wise supplant, for service wear, the strictly tailored suit of this same fabric. And, surprising as it may seem, the utility suit, although practically devoid of novelty, may be made to express an unusual degree of style, provided the foundation lines show the subtle changes in cut that each season requires, even in regulation types, and the workmanship is executed with skill and the greatest care. In perhaps no other type of costume are cut and perfection of detail so essential to successful results as in plain tailored models.

Checked and plain tweed, a combination of merit this season, were selected in very serviceable shades of tan for this design. The jacket is cut on practically straight lines, with a shoulder dart that takes care of the shaping required for the bust and a faced slash at the center back from the waist line to the lower edge that insures ample freedom over the hips.

Wide bindings of the checked fabric finish the collar and the revers, which fall open to the waist line, a feature that is prevalent in spring fashions. Checked bindings also finish the upper edge of the pockets.

The belt of self-material confines some of the waist-line fulness of the jacket, but is not drawn close enough to detract from the straight effect.

The sleeves are long and very close fitting, with just a suggestion of flare at the wrist edge. A short opening in the sleeve is held together by link buttons.

Straight, simple lines characterize the skirt, which is supplied with welt pockets and a narrow belt of self-fabric.

About 2 yards of plain colored fabric 54 inches wide and 1½ yards of the check are required for the average figure, with 2 yards of material for lining.

In order to apply the bindings to the double revers and collar without making a very bulky joining, you may, if you wish, cut fitted instead of bias strips of the checked fabric, shaping these strips so that they correspond to the revers and collar edges, with allowance for a narrow seam on both edges, and arranging the cutting so that the true bias will follow the long edges of the revers and collar. This will necessitate separate trimming strips, one for the upper and one for the under side and, naturally, a seam at the outside edge.

Stitch these strips in position before joining the two portions of the revers and of the collar, trim the seam to a scant ¼ inch, and press it open. Then join the two revers and the two collar portions, each edged with a trimming strip, in the usual manner.

Model 6D.—When a model is cut in a manner such as this, it naturally favors a figure of slender and youthful proportions—the type that is best qualified to bring out its full charm. Poiret twill in Hussar blue, a pure color of medium tone, is the material of which the suit is fashioned.

Short, flaring lines, sleeves of seven-eighths length that repeat the flare and are set into a dropped armhole, an upstanding collar of diminutive form, and embroidery of fine silk braid and heavy silk floss characterize the jacket.

The jacket removed reveals a dress formed by a long-sleeved kimono blouse of white crêpe de Chine joined to the plain skirt of the suit fabric, with straps of this same fabric extending over the blouse in suspender fashion.

The front of the dress, as shown by the illustration in the center of the page, hangs on straight, unrestrained lines, but the back has waist-line fulness confined by a narrow belt. Diamond-shaped sections of the material applied at each side front repeat the embroidery of the jacket.

If you find that the neck opening is not sufficiently large to permit the dress to be slipped over the head, you may make an opening underneath the left front strap.

Average requirements include 3¼ yards of 54-inch fabric, 2 yards of silk for the jacket lining, 2 yards of 40-inch material for the waist portion of the dress, and about 6 skeins of floss, with several yards of very fine braid, the amount depending on the manner in which you use it.

6A

6B

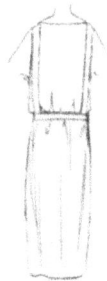

6C

6D

Coats and Capes

Model 7.—Perhaps a bit dashing because of the size of the plaid, but in soft tones of tan and rust that are truly delightful, the heavy novelty woolen of which this model is developed seems just right for the design, which is fashioned on broad, sweeping lines.

Between coats and capes, the style seems somewhat divided in its allegiance, for the bias-cut front bears all the requisites of a coat, while the straight-cut back, except for the semblance of a sleeve that is given by the wide cuff, is to all appearances a cape of broad dimensions. This effect is produced by the front portion of the sleeve being cut in one with the coat front and the back portion of the sleeve formed by the cape, to which the under seam line of the front sleeve portion is slip-stitched and therefore does not make the joining conspicuous.

The skirt portion of the front is extended well under the arm, and the edges are left free from the waist line to the lower edge, being joined by a belt across the back waist line.

Two soft plaits extended from the shoulder seam in both the front and back sections make possible a well-fitted effect over the shoulders with ample fulness below.

The collar, which is of a wide standing type, and the deep cuffs are edged with velour of rust color and the stand portions of the pockets are made of this same material. Composition buttons of rust color arranged in pairs indicate the closing.

A coat of this design requires 4¼ to 4½ yards of plaid fabric 54 inches wide and ¼ yard of plain color. This estimate for the plaid is somewhat greater than would be necessary for a coat of plain material, as allowance must be made for proper arrangement of the plaids.

Model 7A.—When a lining is as prominent as in this design, and especially when it is used with black-and-white checked velour, the neutral color that is the general rule for coat linings must give way to a color having dash and character that compare favorably with the coat fabric. These essentials are included in the bright-red taffeta of very soft quality which lines the cape portion of this model.

Similar in effect to the cape coat considered previously, but with several differences in its development, the design is one that requires extreme care in the development of a muslin model to shape the armhole and sleeve lines properly.

The upper part of the back coat portion is of the lining and is joined to the velour several inches above the waist line.

The cape does not extend over the front coat portion, but is secured to the shoulder line of this. At the end of the shoulder line, however, the cape is extended over the arm to form the entire sleeve and shaped to fit into the front armhole of the coat. As suggested for the other cape coat, the under seam line of the sleeve is slip-stitched to the cape in order that its joining may not be noticeable in the back of the cape.

The collar is of a type that may be turned down and worn low, if desired. The pockets are of the flap variety.

About 5 yards of 54-inch fabric and 5½ yards of lining material are required for a model such as this.

Model 7B.—Spring coat showings include many designs of mannish type with sleeves set into a natural armhole line. Such designs are excellent for utility wear alone, but if one coat must serve for every occasion, it is well to consider the matter of lines before a selection is made in order that the coat will be satisfactory for all purposes.

A model such as this is very desirable from the standpoint of utility as well as style, for the material, homespun in brown and tan, and the simplicity of the design are features that commend it for service wear; and yet these same features keep well within the mode. Provision for the deep armholes that many dresses evidence is made by the smart drop-shoulder line.

The coat is bloused at a low waist line and has a convertible collar that may be worn high or low. The vogue for wide bindings carries them even to the side seam line of the back skirt portion, which is extended in a point below the front.

Double stand pockets, the upper ones merely simulated, and covered buttons repeat the color of the bindings.

For the average figure, provide 4 yards of 54-inch fabric, ⅝ yard of 54-inch contrasting material, and 3½ yards of lining.

Model 7C.—Thoughts of the development of a garment in plaid material need cause no apprehension if a design as simple as this is selected, for the cape is fashioned in shawl effect and consists merely of a straight length of gray plaid of heavy, firm weave about 1 yard wide and 2 yards long.

It is supplied with a bias dart or seam line at the center back, which removes excess length from the upper edge and supplies a note of interest, for the plaids appear perfectly matched in V effect. The neck is shaped a trifle to make the cape fit comfortably. The collar is of gray brushed wool.

Because of the firmness of the weave, the edges of the material, instead of being hemmed or faced, are finished with blanket-stitching of gray yarn taken directly over the cut edges.

Material requirements for the average figure include 2 yards of 36-inch material, ⅝ yard of brushed wool 7 or 8 inches wide, and 4 or 5 small skeins of yarn.

Model 7D.—Can you imagine a collar more fascinating than one made entirely of roses? This is just one of the many delightful features that make the newest silk capes so irresistible. An abundance of shoulder shirrings and a hem finish of deep bound scallops are other points that add to the attractiveness of this model, which is made of gray Canton crêpe.

Like the cape shown in Model 1, this design is made of a straight piece of material, but is 2½ yards in length to provide the width required for a cover-all effect. Very frequently capes of this style also form a part of a three-piece costume, being made of material like that used for the dress and the dress carrying out the trimming of fabric roses, usually across the front waist line.

About 3½ yards of material 40 inches wide is sufficient for the cape, the bindings, the roses, and the fabric cords that tie at the center front. In addition, two long silk tassels are needed as a finish for these cords.

Gauntlet and Mousquetaire Gloves Favored

To be gloved is one thing and to be correctly gloved another, for a surprising bit of smartness can be added to a costume by the choice of gloves that are not only highly favored by Fashion, but also of a style and color that are best for that particular costume.

For spring, kid gloves, both glacé and suède, are becoming increasingly popular, but these will hardly overshadow the fabric glove made in imitation of suède or the silk glove, for leather gloves, except in the more conservative styles, are rather high in price for the big majority of women.

Gauntlet gloves have, if anything, a stronger appeal than ever this year. They are an ideal associate for the jaunty sports suit and, when made in particularly effeminate styles, for tailor-mades of the dressier fabrics. Gauntlet types merge into mousquetaire styles to provide a glove suitable for wear with dresses having sleeves of all lengths.

As to colors, sand, beaver, and mode, which is of drab character, continue their popularity, while gray of the pearl or silver variety is very promising. Spring will undoubtedly bring forth an abundance of all-white and black-trimmed white gloves.

 ©2016 Amy Barickman, LLC

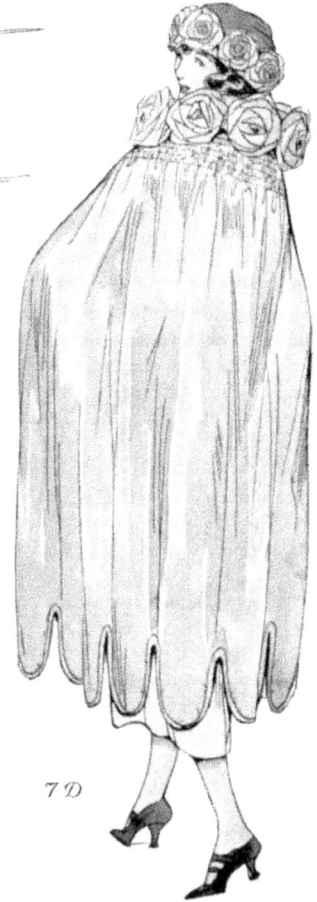

Model 7

7 A

7 B

7 C

7 D

Misses' Costumes

Model 8.—It is said that "good things always come in bunches," and this statement doesn't require any more convincing proof than the winsome maid in her teens, an unlimited variety of fascinating sports apparel from which she may choose, and an entire summer's vacation in which she may revel in her selections.

At least one overblouse style is sure to find its way into the misses' wardrobe, for there is about an overblouse a phase of comfort and utility that makes for freedom and enjoyment in strenuous outdoor activities. This overblouse model, although a straight slip-over style, attains a decidedly bloused effect by means of the broad sash tied closely over a low waist line.

Ratiné is the fabric used for the entire costume, white being the selection for the overblouse and Bermuda, a deep pink ever so slightly tinged with orange, the color of the skirt, sash, and deep-flare cuffs.

The embroidery that decorates the skirt portion of the overblouse is in triangular motifs worked with worsted floss in soft tones of blue, corn color, and green, each row of triangles being of one color. Worsted fringe that matches the fabric in color finishes the sash end.

For the average miss of sixteen, provide 2¼ yards of 36-inch material for the blouse, 2¾ yards of contrasting fabric, and 2 small skeins each of contrasting color in yarn and 5 skeins for the self-colored fringe.

Use a straight-line overblouse pattern with boat-shaped neck line and wide flared sleeves for cutting out the blouse. For the skirt, supply merely straight lengths of material.

Model 8A.—Flared raglan sleeves of seven-eighths length, a low, bloused waist line, a slightly shaped peplum portion, and collar and revers facings of dull fuchsia homespun are the outstanding features of this novel suit of gray homespun. In addition, the jaunty touch provided by the side pockets inserted diagonally above the waist line and the ball buttons covered with the suit fabric and dropped from bound buttonholes are a recognition of youth's appreciation of details.

Provide 3½ yards of 54-inch fabric, with ⅝ yard of contrasting color and 2 yards of lining, for developing this design for the average miss of sixteen.

A jacket pattern having raglan sleeves, a natural neck line with convertible collar, and a bloused or full box effect may be used for the development of this style.

In making the muslin model, if the pattern does not provide the bloused effect, tie a tape over the model at the point you wish the low waist line, draw the muslin down over this to make it blouse as decidedly as you wish, and then cut away the surplus material below the tape.

Model 8B.—In the realm of youth, checked gingham finds a medium of expression that is invariably delightful, for the simplicity that characterizes almost all successful designs for misses provides just the setting for the bright-colored, and sometimes a wee bit audacious, checks of this season.

A vivid green-and-white check and a trimming featuring both these colors, white for the collar and green for the sash and all the bindings, seem to provide just the combination needed to complete the charm and girlishness of this model.

An overdress suggestion is carried in the front portion, the waist being extended into a straight-apron effect edged with bound scallops. The back waist portion extends merely to the waist line, and sash ends brought out at each side front tie at the center back and cover the joining of the skirt and waist. If preferred, however, the back may be cut in one-piece fashion.

Narrow bindings finish the straight sleeves that terminate above the elbow. The shaped, flat collar opened in the back

in line with the waist closing pleasingly sets off the broad neck line, while this, in turn, is given a piquant touch by a small bow of black ciré ribbon placed at the center front.

For an average girl of sixteen, provide 4½ yards 32 inches wide, ¾ yard of contrasting color, and ¼ yard for the collar.

In cutting the front overdress portion, you may use a simple one-piece dress pattern and cut the skirt portion as long as you desire it. Do not shape the lower edge; rather, permit it to follow the straight grain of the material. Then, if the sides appear longer than the center front, remove the surplus length by laying a horizontal dart at the side waist line.

Cut straight pieces for the skirt unless you prefer the back of the dress cut in one piece. In this case, in making the dress, join the side seams of the one-piece back to a straight piece provided for the front portion of the skirt.

Attach the fulness in the front skirt portion to the sash, which may be extended under the center front for a belt, or finish the waist line with a casing and draw elastic through this.

Model 8C.—Another season of dotted Swiss is bound to receive a very enthusiastic welcome, for there are any number of possibilities in its development as yet untouched.

This model is just one of the examples of what Fashion has to offer in dotted Swiss. It is of navy blue made very summery in appearance by its broad sash of crisp white organdie and this same fabric repeated in the narrow collar and cuffs and the bands that trim the sides of the waist and skirt. Embroidery in dainty spray effect trims these bits of organdie, but if this work would require more time than you feel you can afford, you may substitute machine-embroidered organdie banding and edging.

Before attempting to combine white organdie with the navy Swiss, you will do well to test the fastness of the color in the Swiss. If you find that it has a tendency to run even after you have tried to set the color, choose blue organdie rather than white for trimming. This will look very well but will not be quite so attractive as the white. In the end, however, you will be better satisfied, for white trimming that shows streaks of color is bound to detract from the daintiness of the dress.

You will need 3½ to 4 yards of Swiss and 1 yard of material for trimming this dress as illustrated.

In making this model, shape the collar the same as the neck line of the dress so that it will lie flat when it is applied, unless you use edging, which may be fitted by gathers or plaits.

To secure the trimming bands to the waist and skirt, have them machine hemstitched or merely stitch them in position and, after trimming away the surplus material underneath, turn or roll and whip tiny hems under the lines of stitching.

Model 8D.—Fashioned of peach-colored voile with ruffles of fine Val lace grouped in the most fascinating manner, this model is one that would grace the smartest of garden parties or, on the other hand, prove entirely correct for church wear.

With the exception of the groups of pin tucks at each side in the front and back and a simple fitted collar with a double edging of narrow Val, the waist portion is very simple. The sleeves are trimmed in surplice fashion with double rows of Val.

The straight two-piece skirt is relieved of its plainness by side front panels cut 7 or 8 inches wide and trimmed with wider Val in groups of closely laid ruffles.

A sash of narrow harmonizing ribbon covers the joining of the skirt and waist, and roses made of this same ribbon extend across the center-front portion of the sash. For this ribbon, self-material or satin might be substituted, if desired.

Generally, 4 yards of 36- or 40-inch material, 6 yards of narrow and 12 yards of wider lace, and 6 or 7 yards of ribbon are required for the development of this model.

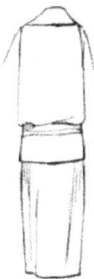

Model 8

8 A

8 D

8 B   8 C

Vintage Notions Monthly   ©2016 Amy Barickman, LLC

Slenderizing Costume

Every woman of generous proportions seems to experience a period when she would make tremendous sacrifices for slenderness; then, just as surely, there will come a time when she realizes that health and happiness are more desirable than willowyness. Her pride, however, never permits her to settle into a state of fatness, even if she must admit to a robustness that is quite genuine.

Stouts, as they are often pictured, are not pleasing, and a self-respecting woman will not admit herself into such a class. We, therefore, have purposely avoided illustrating the stout figure and have endeavored to show lines that will become her.

Long lines are essential. A soft, graceful fabric with enough weight in itself not to be in the least flimsy is always desirable. Sleeves should be plain, and never long if they can be avoided, because if the sleeve is long and loose, the arm appears too heavy. If it is long and fitted in at the wrist, the hand and the upper arm appear to disadvantage. Therefore, the very modest three-quarter sleeve is to be desired.

A simple, unadorned neck line is, in many instances, to be preferred, for if the neck is not wrinkled with flesh, it usually is attractive. If it is wrinkled, then a collar line would make it seem crowded and overdressed. So simplicity is in both instances the safest.

A skirt 1½ to 2½ inches longer is always desirable for one of large proportions, because it intensifies height when one is standing and makes one appear more graceful when sitting.

For the model illustrated, Roshanara crêpe in Mocha color—a medium tan—was selected. The dress is a one-piece model having a dart line from the hip to the shoulder in the front and panel lines the full length of the back. Covering the termination of the dart lines and extending to the lower edge of the skirt are strips of material applied in panel effect. These are stitched flat to the skirt, with the exception of the upper ends, which are left open and have a row of stitching placed about 4 inches below them to provide pockets.

Outlining the panels are three rows of wool darning-stitches in red, green, and violet, which leave unfinished ends to extend below the skirt hem in a suggestion of fringe. Corresponding rows of darning-stitches are run in vertical lines in the lower edge of the otherwise plain, slightly flared sleeve.

At the center front of the waist, the material is cut away to permit the use of a narrow vest of cream-colored satin. This breaks the broad effect that the square neck line would give.

A jade buckle finishes the narrow belt of self-material which but loosely confines the waist-line fulness.

Such materials as Canton crêpe, silk or cotton ratiné, Kasha cloth, and the fine woolen twills are all suitable for this model.

Material and Pattern Requirements.—For the average stout figure, provide 4 yards of material 36 or 40 inches wide, and 1 small skein of each of the three colors of yarn. The vest requires a strip of material 3 or 4 inches wide and 12 to 15 inches long.

A one-piece dress pattern having a side-front dart and a full-length back panel is needed for cutting the design. If this does not have a vest portion, you may outline one in developing the muslin model. Especially in the development of a one-piece dress for a stout figure is extreme care required in the making of a muslin model, for oftentimes a slight change in the fitting will necessitate a more decided change on some other seam line, which could not be made in the dress itself without marring its appearance.

You will undoubtedly find it possible to cut the skirt trimming bands from strips of material left from the full-length dress portions. Cut these about 5 inches wide and long enough to extend from several inches below the waist line to the lower edge of the skirt, plus the same allowance as that made for the dress hem, unless you are using material that would make the several thicknesses at the lower edge too bulky. Mark-stitch the lines for the panels on the dress material as a guide in the making.

Making.—Baste the darts and seams of the dress with close stitches. Then try it on to make sure that it fits correctly in every detail before you stitch any of the seam lines.

After stitching the darts, press the edges together back on the center-front portion and finish these edges with overcastings.

Before applying the straps to the front portion, face the upper ends, which are intended for the pockets, with pieces of light-weight silk or with self-material, provided this is not too heavy. Make these facings ½ inch deeper than you desire the pocket and, when applying them, stitch ½-inch seams at the sides, for a ½-inch turn must be made on the strap edges below the pocket.

After facing the upper ends of the straps, turn under the edges and press them. Then apply the rows of darning-stitches, leaving the yarn ends free at the point where you consider the hem turn will come. Next, baste them to the skirt portion so that they follow the lines marked for them.

Finish the shoulder, under-arm, and sleeve seams by pressing them open and overcasting them. But instead of pressing open the armhole and back-panel seams, press the armhole edges together back on the panel. Then overcast these edges.

Apply narrow facings to the front and neck edges of the waist portion of the dress. If you wish to accentuate these edges, you may secure the inner edge of the facing with stitching; otherwise, use hemming-stitches for this purpose. Also, face the lower edge of the sleeves.

Make the double belt, but do not finish the ends until the dress is on the figure and you can determine by experiment what length will prove most satisfactory.

While the dress is on the figure so that the belt length may be determined, pin the strip for the vest in position and also turn the skirt hem.

Finishing.—Secure the hem in the skirt with loose, fine whipping stitches. Then secure the straps with slip-stitching, taking these stitches 1/16 inch or so back from the edge so that they will not make the edge appear drawn and supplying an occasional back-stitch to make the straps very secure.

If the darning-stitches that decorate the straps run beyond the hem turn, pull out the surplus and cut the ends even.

Complete the dress by applying darning-stitches to the sleeves, slip-stitching the right edge of the vest and finishing the left side for a closing, and securing the end of the belt to the buckle.

Neck Finishes Show Variety

With the bateau, or boat-shaped, neck line still receiving so much emphasis in fashion articles, one is led to wonder whether any other neck finish is considered really smart. But, truly, there is an agreeable variety in neck lines, for this variety is essential in a day when we are trained to recognize the neck finish as probably the most important detail of a costume in so far as its individual becomingness is concerned.

Neck lines tend to conservatism, for the collarless mode is still a dominating note. And of the collarless neck lines, the bateau shape is undoubtedly the most frequently followed. But the deep round neck, the V effect, and the square outline, each has its representation in spring and summer styles, the square neck usually being accompanied by a vestee and a collar.

Model 9

Variations of Slenderizing Costume

Model 9A.—A limp, very fine weave of silk jersey having an even stripe of cactus green and white is the material used to accentuate the long lines of this model. Besides the influence of the fabric, which is employed with such skill, the points in the skirt, the long collar, the cuff line, and the wee tucks above the waist line, all are worthy of attention, for each does its bit in accomplishing the slender silhouette.

White crêpe satin forms the collar and the band that finishes the upper edge of the vest. The frills, also, are of this fabric.

Not only jersey, but other silks, as well as voiles and tissue ginghams woven in narrow stripes, fairly invite one to make them up in a design such as this.

Provide, for the average stout figure, 5½ yards of material 36 or 40 inches wide and ⅝ yard of contrasting fabric for trimming.

In making the dress, so as to eliminate as much waist-line fulness as possible in the underskirt, use a fitted lining for the upper back portion, letting this extend just a trifle in front of the side seam line. Also, to permit the stripes to extend in an even line around the lower edge, hang the underskirt from the waist line.

Model 9B.—In addition to its summeryness, this dress is blessed with two other assets—dignity and smartness. In printed voile with plain voile bands, the dress design has many possibilities, but it might also be developed with excellent results from plain-colored silk crêpe or voile.

The semi-raglan line is good for breaking the width. The surplice front with long collar line and the sleeve with its interesting trimming band, all tend to make this an especially good type for a plump or overplump figure.

As illustrated, the model is made of navy and white foulard having a design of rather indistinct outline, which makes it especially desirable for a generously proportioned figure. Double folds of Georgette crêpe edge the panels and sleeves and indicate the low waist line, and a single thickness accentuates the raglan lines in the waist. The collar and vest of white organdie may be omitted and the dark trimming material substituted when a simpler dress is desired.

For the average stout figure, provide 6 yards of 36- or 40-inch material, 1 yard for the trimming bands, and ¾ yard for the collar and vest.

In applying double folds of Georgette, you will find that straight pieces can be used with good results for the straight edges. But for the shaped waist-line edge, a bias strip will prove more satisfactory. With care, this may be applied to the waist so that it shapes correctly and does not bulge at any point.

Model 9C.—Dotted gray voile and pin-tucked, plain white voile are combined in a delightful way in this model. The pin tucks take away every wee bit of monotony in the dress, and they serve, also, to keep the long-line effect in a very pleasing way.

Figured or plain voile or dotted Swiss might be substituted for the dotted voile. Then, too, any number of pleasing color combinations might be effected, brown, blue, or cypress green with tan, or mulberry with a lighter tone of the same color, immediately suggesting possibilities.

Because of the manner in which the front and back panels break the appearance of width in the waist portion of the design, the kimono sleeves will not prove objectionable for most stout figures. If you feel, however, that the slight bagginess that is essential in a kimono sleeve would prove unbecoming or that the width of the shoulders needs a more definite slenderizing influence, do not hesitate to provide for set-in sleeves, as they will not mar the lines of the dress.

Average requirements for the stout figure include 4 yards of figured material and 1¾ yards of plain color.

After cutting off a piece of material for the vestee of the dress and narrow collar and cuff bindings, you will find it advantageous to tuck the full width of the material before cutting the pieces for the other sections. Use the sewing-machine tucking attachment for this purpose, adjusting it for the narrowest possible tuck and for spacing of the width you desire.

By finishing the edges of the collar and cuffs with a very narrow self-binding, you will provide a neat, durable finish that will prove more satisfactory than picoting and more attractive than narrow or full facings.

Apply the tucked bands to the side-skirt sections before joining them to the front and back panels, securing these bands by stitching or by having them machine hemstitched. Also join the collar and cuffs to the waist in a like manner.

Model 9D.—Tissue gingham or dainty Georgette, the choice depending on the purpose, is the suggestion offered by this design. Either one is admirable for this type and will make a dress that can be worn throughout the summer with delight and satisfaction.

The Tuxedo front, which is enhanced by the belt arrangement, should be gauged in width for individual becomingness. The cuff gives a right emphasis to the sleeve, and the buttons centered in the vest attract the eye and break the figure in a right way.

Corresponding with the front skirt panels, into which the Tuxedo collar is extended, are applied panels at each side back, these extending a trifle above the waist line and being finished with a row of buttons.

Blue-and-white tissue gingham combined with plain blue chambray of an extremely fine, soft quality are the fabrics used for the dress, as illustrated. The buttons are covered with the chambray, bone molds forming the foundation, as these withstand laundering and do not discolor the fabric.

About 4 yards of gingham and 2 yards of chambray are required for developing this model for the average stout figure. In addition, 2½ dozen small and 2 dozen larger button molds are needed.

Model 9E.—The firm gracefulness of Canton crêpe and trimming applied in such a way as to give perfect lines unite in making this a model of enviable distinction and suitability. Just as a fat man must always have a good tailor, so a stout woman must ever insist on neatly made clothes, and must permit of ornament only when its application is perfection personified.

Bronze beads applied in narrow-band effect provide the long trimming lines that edge the sleeve bands and the full-length front and back panels and extend in triple rows the full length of the front panel. Much of the fulness of the panels is concentrated at the sides, where it is held by several short rows of shirring placed just below the waist line. The belt, which but loosely confines the waist-line fulness, terminates at each side front. Here, the ends are finished with bronze ornaments, from which are suspended bronze-colored silk tassels—a detail that enters into the trimming of the sleeve band, also.

The collar, which is of a narrow, standing type, is especially new and worthy of attention, for it befriends the neck and adds length to the dress in a constructive way. It might be used with good effect for Model 9, provided the neck line were shaped in V fashion.

This model requires, for the average stout figure, 6 yards of material 40 inches wide, 16 bunches of beads, and ½ dozen silk tassels. If you prefer, you may substitute very light-weight beaded banding or fancy braid for the hand beading.

9A

9B

9C

9D

9E

Home Dresses

Husbands and fathers often prefer to see their womenfolk in dainty, fresh home dresses than in any other type, and there is indeed a beautiful sentiment about an attractive gingham or print dress that has lasted through many years. It seems, when it is possible to give so much pleasure by means of a lovely wash dress, that it is almost sacreligious to wear an untidy or unbecoming one.

Bright colors that will look well after washing are delightful for home dresses if they are becoming. A home dress, in addition to its becomingness, must be neat and homey. An offensive color hinders these two factors and should be definitely avoided. But there is an ocean of pretty colors of good dye that are becoming, yet not intrusive. Rose, lavender, and many pinks, grays, yellows, tans, and blues are wonderfully attractive alone and often extremely smart when combined.

The most modest shops boast of unusually pretty patterns in ginghams, chambrays, prints, crêpes, and the like, and it is well, too, to remember that in the small shop or store the daintiest pieces are often to be found, because in a "one-man store" the selection is usually made piece by piece and, consequently, a better selection is possible than when case lots are purchased and the crude patterns are in the majority.

Always, in home dresses, one must think of the laundering, because one of the chief charms of such a dress lies in its absolute freshness. Some home-efficiency engineers said seersucker dresses and tried definitely to promote them, but they lacked neatness and were tabooed by the discriminating housewife.

But a generous compromise is to be had in Japanese crêpe, especially the medium and good grades, which cost 35 to 50 cents a yard. This fabric is usually 32 inches wide. It launders very well and requires only smoothing out, no starch, and thorough ironing. Also, it comes in many colors, one for every whim.

'Tis easy to sew, and surprisingly good results may be attained by one quite new at sewing if a good pattern is at hand and careful stitching is done throughout.

Model 10.—This slip-over model is of Japanese crêpe, the original in orange color, with a reddish tobacco-brown trimming. The combination is unusual and pleasing for one who has a clear complexion and hair that can permit of the orange glow.

For summer, the dress in pink with trimming of white, or gray with trimming of pink is pleasing. The dress may also be embroidered daintily in a color to correspond with the trimming, or the bindings may be the same as the dress and the contrast used only in the embroidery.

For this dress, 4½ yards of material is required, with ¾ yard of contrasting color for the bindings and button coverings.

Provide, for the blouse, a long-waisted kimono sleeve pattern that has a panel front and back. To have the center front and center back on a straight grain of the material is important in crêpe, for it insures a garment that will "set" rightly when on; also, one that will retain its correct shape after it is laundered.

For the skirt, cut two full widths of material of the skirt length, measured from the low waist line, plus allowance for a hem.

Cut pieces 7 inches long and 8 inches wide for the pockets, and then shape the upper edge. For the sash, cut two strips, each 1¼ yards long and 6 inches wide.

As all the bindings except those used for the pockets are applied to practically straight edges, you may cut them lengthwise of the material and a scant 1 inch wide, for straight bindings are easier to apply than bias ones. Cut bias bindings for the pockets, however, as these are needed on curved edges.

After making sure that the panel widths are becoming, bind both lengthwise edges of the front and back panels, the lower edge of the front panel, and also the long edges and one end of each strip provided for the sash. Gather the raw end of each sash portion and baste it to the front panel. Then join the side waist sections to the panels by laying the bound panel edges over the edges of the side sections so that a seam's width extends underneath the panels and stitching close to the binding, securing the sash ends, also, with this stitching.

Seam the skirt and gather the waist line. Then join this to the lower edge of the waist in a plain seam, letting the lower portion of the front panel extend down over the skirt.

Complete the dress by turning and securing the skirt hem, binding the neck and sleeve edges, binding and applying the pockets, and sewing self-covered buttons to the front panel.

Model 10A.—Miss Modesty seems the right name for this model, which is developed of tissue gingham in white and soft, green plaid, with a matching green voile as trimming. Lace, if desired, may be substituted for the voile, and set on rather than set in, as lace usually is. In such an event, a bias sash of the dress material would necessarily be used.

The daintiness of this dress gives it possibilities in many materials, especially voile, organdie, dimity, Swiss, etc.

Average material requirements for this model include 4½ yards of plaid and 1 yard of plain color.

For cutting out the waist, use a plain-waist pattern having a straight vest portion and straight set-in sleeves. No patterns are needed for the collar and cuffs, as these are merely straight pieces of material. Cut the strips for these 7 inches wide, this including allowance for a ¾-inch hem. Make the collar strip of a length sufficient to extend around the neck line and down each side to a low waist line, and the cuff strips 1½ or 2 inches longer than the measurement of the lower edge of the sleeves.

Cut two full widths of material for the skirt, and, for the sash, cut straight strips about 6 inches wide and of a length that, when seamed together, will be 2½ or 3 yards.

For the trimming bands, cut strips about 2 inches wide.

To apply the trimming bands, turn under both edges and stitch close to these turned edges. Arrange the bands on the collar and cuffs so that the stitching of the outside edge of the band will catch the edge of the ¾-inch hems.

Before applying the cuffs, stitch the ends in a bias seam to make the cuff flare a trifle. To make the collar fit properly around the neck, fold in tiny plaits at the back neck line.

Arrange the skirt seams so that one will fall at the right side front and the other at the left side back, each at the inside edge of the plaits that indicate the panel lines. By turning under the ends of the side trimming bands exactly even with the inside edge of the plaits, the joining will not be conspicuous.

Join the waist and skirt to a soft inside belting, and have the sash picoted or bind it with the trimming material.

Trimmings Giving Way to Fabric Combinations

This season the fad for combining materials precludes the use of trimming in many models, for the two or sometimes three and even four fabrics in combination provide sufficient decorative effect in themselves.

As summed up in general, plain contrasting colors are used together; figured, striped, checked, or plaid, with plain colors; smooth weaves, with rough weaves; dull finishes, with lustrous surfaces; sheer fabrics, with heavy ones; cotton or linen, with silk; and silk, with wool. The principal thought in combinations seems to be a decided difference in nature, for those which sharply contrast demand particular interest.

10 a

Model 10

Variations of Home Dress

Model 10B.—In debate, 'twould be difficult to say whether neatness or becomingness would be most evident in this dress, especially if made up, as the original was, in soft, green chambray gingham with trimming of checked gingham in green and white, a wee black moiré ribbon bow, and smart pearl buttons.

This is a good style for two colors of linen, one color being used for the dress and a lighter color for the vest, collar, and sleeve trimming.

For the average figure, provide 3½ yards of 36-inch material, with ½ yard of the same width for the vest, collar, and sleeve trimmings.

In finishing the collar, use a facing that will be about ¾ inch wide when applied, and secure this with stitching or have it machine hemstitched. Also, turn hems of this same width in the sleeve trimmings and have them finished in a similar manner.

Model 10C.—Some one had a happy idea in creating the applied designs for gingham, for they are smart and different, and make excellent trimming for children's as well as grown-ups' dresses.

The upper portion of this dress is of deep pink, with a pink-and-white checked skirt and trimming. It may also be made in lavender, with lavender-and-white trimming, or in green, yellow, gray, or blue. The mood and the scolding lock may be matched for color in such a dress. It also has the girlishness to button up the back, giving a youthful line so often desirable.

Provide 1½ yards of plain and 2⅛ yards of checked material for the average figure.

To make the appliqué trimming, which is shown in enlarged detail at the left of the dress, mark designs of the shape illustrated on pieces of the material and have machine hemstitching done on these lines. After cutting the hemstitching in two to form a picoted edge, appliqué to the center of each a smaller petaled section cut from plain material, securing its edges with blanket-stitches and working French knots at the center.

Model 10D.—Smart enough in design for business wear, yet womanly enough to be entirely at home in domestic surroundings, this dress of burlap-colored, fine Japanese crêpe has for its principal decoration embroidery worked in a harmonizing tone of brown mercerized floss.

An enlarged detail of the embroidery is shown at the extreme right of the page of illustrations. The central portion of this consists of small stitches laid in pairs in alternating horizontal and vertical positions, and these stitches are connected by threads drawn through them in a manner similar to the twisted running-stitch. This central row is bordered on one side with darning-stitches in zigzag effect, and on the other side with outlining-stitches.

By omitting the linen collar and continuing the embroidery of the front up and around the neck, you may simplify the design, or you may even omit the embroidery and use a binding of the same material in matching or contrasting color.

A novelty feature is in the waist line. 'Tis a one-piece chemise dress, you know, and has a waist-line casing 1¼ inches wide, through which a sash of ribbon or of the contrasting trimming material is run, so that it can be drawn up and tied at the sides and the blouse effect produced.

About 4½ yards of material 36 inches wide, 4½ yards of ribbon, and 3 or 4 skeins of floss are generally required.

Model 10E.—This design was created especially for Mae Marsh when she took the part of a dainty little sweetheart who kept house. It is of lavender-and-white checked gingham, with white handkerchief-linen collar, vest, sleeve and pocket bands and cross-stitch embroidery of a rich purple.

It is as quick as a minute in smartness and unusually becoming to many types; also, it is as pretty in plain as in check material.

For the average figure, 3¾ yards of material 36 inches wide is sufficient for this model. For the trimming, ¼ yard of contrasting material and 4 or 5 skeins of floss are needed.

Model 10F.—This model, which is suitable for slender figures only, is a real inspiration in a home dress. It is developed of printed cotton having a white ground well covered with a dainty yellow flower; then a plain-yellow chambray gingham serves as trimming.

The dress slips over the head, has a 6½-inch opening down the center back, and is as easy to iron as a simple night dress, for when the sash is undone the dress lies out flat, the sash alone holding the dress in place at the waist line.

Material requirements for the average figure include 2¾ yards of figured and 1¾ yards of plain fabric.

Model 10G.—This is a copy of a "store model," but such a popular one that we are giving it here. Merchants say that when this is seen by a housewife, 'tis purchased immediately.

A kimono night-dress pattern with sleeves can actually serve for cutting the dress part, for the "bib" and sash combination is a separate piece held in place by the two buttons underneath the "bib" at each side of the neck line.

The dress is cut down at the center front, so that it can be slipped over the head easily. Then when the front piece is buttoned, the opening is entirely concealed.

For the ironing, the front sash piece may be removed and all can be laid out entirely flat.

A figured material is smart, but this should not be over-heavy; percale, for instance, is a bit too stiff, while chambray or French gingham is admirable. A finishing edge of rick-rack, scalloping, or bias binding is good, or if the dress is of plain material, the edges may be bound with self-material and a smart design of embroidery in triangles or patchwork applied to the upper part of the front piece for decoration.

About 4 yards of material is required for the average figure, and 5 yards of trimming, if applied as illustrated.

Model 10H.—Bright navy batiste in plain color and figured navy and white printed cotton are the fabrics of which this youthful model is fashioned. It is a slip-over, flat waist-line finished dress that takes but an afternoon to make, and is one that can be worn with thorough satisfaction.

To develop this dress for the average figure, provide 2¼ yards of plain and 1⅜ yards of figured material, with 2½ to 3 yards of rickrack for trimming.

In making the dress, you will find little or no fitting necessary if the pattern size is correct. You may apply the neck and sleeve trimming before stitching the under-arm seams, thus making it possible to accomplish the work neatly and quickly.

Model 10I.—Except for the material and trimming, the front of this dress is but little different in appearance from Model 10H. The back, however, is cut without a waist-line seam, and its straight fulness is confined somewhat with sash ends tied at the center back.

A soft, gray cotton printed with a rose-ring design and white-lawn sleeve and pocket bands and neck binding are the materials used. This dress also slips over the head, spreads flat for ironing, and requires little fitting. Its simplicity makes a good color choice imperative and a medium firm fabric desirable.

Average requirements include 3¼ yards of material and ¼ yard for trimming the dress as illustrated.

10 C

10 D

10 E

10 B

10 F

10 G

10 H

10 I

Blouses and Skirts

Model 11.—A summer wardrobe that does not include an overblouse of the utility type is surely not complete. Such a blouse is ideal not only as a means of "wearing out" a skirt that is considered unsuitable for street wear, but also as a saver of laundry work; besides, it has noteworthy comfort-giving qualities in its simple roominess.

Cretonne in which yellow is the predominating color is the material that trims this kimono-sleeved model of yellow cotton crêpe. The wide, straight band at the lower edge of the blouse is stitched to the blouse across the center front and center back, but is stitched separately at the sides to form roomy pockets.

Worn with a skirt that matches the trimming material, this model would make an unusually attractive costume.

About 2¼ yards of crêpe and ¼ yard of cretonne are needed.

Model 11A.—There is no need for a white linen blouse to be at all concerned about bringing originality into its cut when a few deft touches of rose can provide so much individuality.

A double band of the rose accents the front opening, which is secured by fabric-covered loops and buttons. This same idea is carried in the bands that trim the puff sleeves. "Finger" pockets add what seems to be the final note of perfection.

Average material requirements include 1¾ yards of white and ½ yard of contrasting color, each 36 to 40 inches wide.

Model 11B.—A frilled blouse and a trim tailored suit—what more desirable combination for spring could one want? Voile is the material chosen for this model, white for the main portion and blue for the bindings that finish the collar, frills, and cuffs. Simple hand-drawn work adds further decoration and makes a very lovely trimming; but it might be omitted if a very simple style is preferred. Slight shoulder fulness of the front waist portion is taken care of by groups of pin tucks.

For the average figure, provide 2¼ yards of material for the blouse and ⅜ yard of contrasting color for bindings.

Model 11C.—Peppermint red stripes the white silk of this sports blouse in such a manner that the fabric resembles in no small degree the stick candy from which the color borrowed its name. Further emphasis is laid on this color by the rows of stitching that outline the side closing and front neck line and by the buttons arranged in groups at the ends of the closing.

The collar and cuffs are of sheer white linen edged with Val. The belt consists of simply a double straight band made according to a measurement taken very loosely over a low waist line.

For most figures, 2 yards of silk, ½ yard of material for the collar and cuffs, and 2¾ yards of Val are sufficient.

Model 11D.—Yoke and upper sleeve portions cut in one, besides adding to the novelty of this design, provide an opportunity for the use of two kinds of fabrics. And when two materials are used together this season, one of them may exhibit polka dots as a very smart note in the newest silk. Crêpe de Chine in canna color and in white dotted with canna were chosen in this instance, and a rosette of canna-colored ribbon applied to the straight double belt.

This model requires, for the average figure, 1⅝ yards of figured material, 1¾ yards of 40-inch fabric, and 1¾ yards of 1-inch ribbon.

Model 11E.—A blouse of green-and-white checked gingham and a separate skirt and sleeveless overblouse of green spongeen —a new material of homespun weave—are combined to form this simple but nevertheless striking three-piece costume. Plaited frills of green lawn trim the collar and black ciré braid finishes all the edges of the overblouse, which is fashioned on very plain lines with Tuxedo collar and revers. The skirt is a straight two-piece model gathered at the waist line.

To develop this costume as illustrated, provide 2½ yards of material for the blouse, with ⅜ yard for frills, and 3¾ yards of 36-inch fabric for the skirt and overblouse, with 6 yards of braid.

Model 11F.—The long lines afforded by the side front and back panels of this skirt of tan Prunella make it particularly desirable for one whose proportions require slenderizing styles.

This is a two-piece model having slight waist-line fulness at the sides and across the back. The back panels are stitched from the waist to the hip line, and from this point to the lower edge they are finished separate from the skirt. The front panels terminate several inches below the waist line and are finished as pockets at the upper end; then, from the pockets, narrow double straps extend to the waist line.

About 2¼ yards of material 44 to 54 inches in width is needed for this style.

Model 11G.—Blanket, or wrap-around, skirts are the last word in fashion so far as tweed and homespun models are concerned, and almost invariably skirts made in this manner are fringed at the lower edge in lieu of a hem.

This wrap-around model is of tweed in gray flaked with rich purple and black. Simulated buttonholes placed diagonally and completed with large self-covered buttons break the long line of the closing.

For a skirt a trifle less than 1½ yards in width, a few inches more than a skirt length, usually 1⅛ yards of 54-inch fabric, will be sufficient.

To make the fringe, have a row of machine hemstitching run around the lower edge at the depth you wish the fringe from the bottom. Then fray out the material.

Model 11H.—The suspender skirt, just a shade away from the guimpe, or sleeveless, dress of last season, comes in many pleasing variations this year. Some of these skirts are cut in abbreviated one-piece dress fashion, but others, like this model, have the waist, or suspender, portion separate.

Blue wool is the fabric of this design, but cotton homespun might be used with good effect. Dull-metal buckles fasten the straps to the front "bib" portion and, placed at each side front of the waist line, provide a means of adjusting the belt.

The skirt is a straight two-piece model cut away at the sides to form distended hip pockets, which are trimmed with large self-covered buttons.

Worn with the suspender skirt is a simple blouse of white habutaye silk. The center portion of the sleeve is slashed its full length and the edges are bound and merely tacked together at the elbow.

For the average figure, it will be necessary to provide 2 yards of 54-inch fabric for the suspender skirt and 1¾ yards of 36- or 40-inch material for the waist.

White Sweaters Carry the Day

If Palm Beach preferences are taken as a forerunner of the summer sweater vogue, as they will be, white sweaters will have an unusual run of popularity. The all-white sweater in wool or silk, most often in fine Shetland, seems most promising, although trimming of black and less frequently of colors is also shown.

This does not mean that the colored sweater has had its day for, in addition to white, a notable range of colors, both somber and gay, in plain, plaid, striped, or figured effects, are evident.

The slip-on and Tuxedo are still the leading styles, and whether one may choose either or both types is a matter of one's proportions and the purpose for which the model is intended.

Medium lengths prevail, hip-length being the general rule.

11A

11B

Model 11

11C   11D

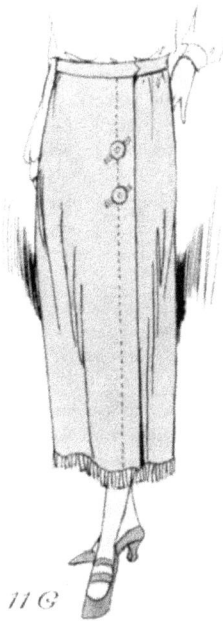

11E   11F   11G   11H

Junior Fashions

Model 12.—One's clothes problems begin in earnest when the time for graduation from grammar school approaches, for surely, on a day when one's mentality is proclaimed sufficiently developed for high-school work, one's frock should bear out this evidence of mature judgment by being entirely correct.

A style just right for such an important occasion is found in this model of white voile. Groups of pin tucks form the full-length front and back panel effects and petal-like side draperies edged in narrow Val provide the fluffiness that is such a coveted quality in junior fashions.

The ribbon sash may be of white or of a pastel color, according to whether or not the color is permissible for this particular purpose. At any rate, a colored sash to which a few dainty rosebuds are secured at the side front is especially desirable for most dress-up occasions.

For the average girl of 14 years, 3¼ yards of material 36 or 40 inches wide, 10 to 12 yards of lace, and 2½ yards of ribbon are needed.

Before cutting out the material for this dress, arrange the tucks for the front and back panel effects, or, if you feel that the making of the tucks will require too much time, you may omit them and make the model somewhat simpler.

In applying the petals, lay them back over the skirt and stitch along the upper edge; then let them drop over the stitching so as to conceal it.

Model 12A.—Frills aplenty convert this simple one-piece model of tile-blue linen into a street frock that would delight even the most fastidious young person.

Fine white linen is the contrasting material employed. This forms a full-length front panel about 1½ inches wide and is studded with linen-covered buttons and edged with ¾-inch frills. The collar and the cuffs in modified mousquetaire style are edged with 2½-inch frills.

If you prefer to make this dress with short sleeves, it will be well to omit the low drop-shoulder effect and extend the sleeves in kimono fashion, or set the sleeves into a natural or only slightly dropped armhole line.

Imitation linen, chambray, cotton homespun, and gingham, combined with lawn or organdie, are other possibilities for this design. Also, gathered rather than plaited frilling might be used.

For the average girl of twelve, supply 2¾ yards of 36-inch material and 1 yard of a contrasting color for trimming.

Model 12B.—For one's very first suit, what smarter could one choose than a three-piece model of tweed—solid rose color in the skirt, waist trimming, and collar of the jacket, and a plaid, alternated by black-and-white stripes in the jacket?

The short box coat, which is flared just enough to emphasize the youthfulness of the wearer, does not choose to rely on the novelty of its material alone to direct attention from the extremely plain skirt, for it adds flat cordings of black taffeta to simulate triple graduated pockets on each front, narrow straps and small rosettes to the sleeves, and wider straps and a Windsor tie to the collar.

The waist of the dress, as illustrated at the lower right, is of white crêpe de Chine made in drop-shoulder effect, with peasant sleeves and a round neck and side waist opening accented by bands of the skirt material.

A girl of fourteen requires 1⅛ yards of plain-colored fabric and 1⅜ yards of plaid, both 54 inches wide, with ¾ yard of silk for trimming and 1¾ yards for a lining, if one is desired.

Cut all the taffeta trimmings on a true bias, first cutting the width and length required for the tie, usually 5 or 6 inches in width and 1 yard in length, unless it is to be extended around the neck, in which case ¼ yard extra must be provided.

Stitch or slip-stitch the strap trimming in position. For the pockets, make straps of a double thickness and apply these to the coat in pairs, letting the folded edges just meet and stitching or slip-stitching merely the seamed or outer edges to the coat.

Model 12C.—Too much cannot be said of the charm of sheer summer fabrics for the feminine world in general. But for the young girl in particular, they may be made especially fascinating, for tucks and ruffles and lace and ribbons, all trimmings of the kind that enhance these fabrics, may be used in profusion so far as youth is concerned.

A rather light-green Swiss dotted with soft ecru is the material employed in this instance. Ecru insertion and lace finish the neck and sleeve edges, and a sash of narrow velvet ribbon of darker green than the material indicates the low waist line.

At each side front, extending from the neck line for 3 or 4 inches are groups of pin tucks. The entire skirt, with the exception of the deep hem, is covered with gathered bias ruffles placed in horizontal overlapping rows.

You may prefer to cut the ruffles crosswise of the material rather than bias. Bias ruffles have a soft, pleasing effect, but unless ironed with the greatest care are apt to vary in width.

Provide 4½ yards of 36-inch material, 1¼ yards of insertion, 2¾ yards of lace, and 2½ yards of ribbon for the average girl of fourteen years.

Model 12D.—Not only to add picturesque notes to beach or mountain resort, but also to provide cheery spots of color in drab urban surroundings and make the city a pleasanter habitation during sultry summer days, are excellent reasons for the adoption of bright cretonne frocks such as this. And besides, cretonne frocks have become astonishingly prevalent in the wardrobes of one's elders!

Orange, blue, green, and fuchsia colorings are predominant in this cretonne, and just enough black to set off these colors with unusual character is evident. The plain colored material is of green chambray, and on this, at the neck and sleeve edges, the note of black is repeated in bindings of sateen.

The dress is a simple one-piece, kimono-sleeve model having the rectangular trimming bands machine hemstitched in position and the cretonne cut away underneath them. At the neck and sleeve edges a single thickness of the chambray is applied and the outer edge of this finished with the binding.

In the choice and application of trimmings lies much of the success of a cretonne dress, for unless they are selected with a regard for the color that enhances the figured fabric and used in just the right amount, they will not prove satisfactory.

Generally, 2½ yards of cretonne and ½ yard of trimming material are sufficient for a twelve-year-old girl.

Model 12E.—Gingham, the ever-dependable fabric of childhood, does not have an opportunity to become monotonous when each season brings so many new colors and such an abundance of novel designs for its development.

Canna-and-white plaid carries the honors in this little gingham model and, as is so often the case with checked or plaid gingham, the individuality of the design is largely dependent on the use of bias self-material. Separate panels at each side front of the skirt, front and back sashes tied at each under arm, narrow bands that trim the organdie collar, and binding for the center-front opening are detailed uses of the bias. The organdie appears again in the bindings that finish the sleeves and the edges of the slash made in each panel to simulate pockets and in the buttons that outline these slashes.

For the average girl of ten years, provide 3¼ yards of gingham and ⅜ yard of organdie for this style.

12 A

12 B

12 C

Model 12

12 D

12 E

Children's Frocks

Model 13.—If there is any more pleasant sensation than that derived from wearing a party cape of sky-blue taffeta, that sensation comes when one doffs the cape and reveals a frock of fine French voile made in a most bewitching manner and finished on all its edges with bindings that match the cape material.

This little dress, although apparently rather complicated as to design, is really quite simple, for it is a one-piece model, not cut in four separate front and back panels, as one might suppose, but with panel sections indicated by double rows of darning-stitches, one in blue and one in yellow. On the side seam lines, the darning-stitches run from the bottom only as far as the fluffy rosette of blue taffeta ribbon.

Each of the indicated panels is further emphasized by its being cut in deep scallops embroidered in a dainty rosebud design. The very short sleeves also are scalloped.

Any of the soft, sheer cotton fabrics in white or colors are suitable for a design such as this. And even a heavier cotton material, if this be of a very soft quality, such as Japanese crêpe, and in an unusual color, would be lovely embroidered in bright-colored yarns and bound with a contrasting color of this same material or of sateen.

Usually, 2 yards of 36-inch material, ⅜ yard for bindings, and 6 to 8 small skeins of yarn are sufficient for a child of six.

The style of the little cape is especially desirable for taffeta in light or dark colors. It is made of a straight piece of material about 1½ yards long and of a width corresponding to the length you desire the cape to be. This length is used crosswise and gathered at the neck line into a deep roll collar having a fabric rose nestling close to its opening, and at the lower edge, into a straight double band 2½ or 3 inches wide and about 1⅛ yards long, when finished. A lining of soft silk cut the same length as the band and about 2 inches shorter than the cape permits the cape to puff in harem-skirt fashion.

For a six-year-old, 2 yards of taffeta and 1⅛ yards of lining are required.

Model 13A.—Spider-web designs, each apparently suspended by a single thread from the neck and waist line of this model, convert an otherwise plain frock into one of striking individuality.

Fine cotton crêpe in wallflower, a color akin to henna, is the fabric of which the dress is made, and black and white yarn, the floss in which the embroidery is developed.

Each "web" is formed by a series of circular rows of white darning-stitches, one within another, and these circles divided into sections by stitches of the black taken over the circles. Outlining-stitches of black provide the suspension threads.

For the average girl of eight years, provide 2 yards of cotton crêpe, 3 small skeins of white yarn, and 3 of black.

Model 13B.—Princess Mary's favorite "bright-eye" blue would look long before finding a more charming setting than in a frock worn by a winsome blue-eyed lass of tender years. For just such a lass, this blue linen frock is intended, for its simple lines and dainty rosebud embroidery in rose, green, and yellow applied to trimming of white linen are features that she can emphasize and wear with special grace.

The straight lines of the one-piece front are unbroken, save for the belt that extends from the sides across the back.

Material requirements for the girl of eight include 2¼ yards 36 inches wide, ½ yard for trimming, and 6 skeins of floss.

Model 13C.—After one has had but little time or occasion to wear other than school frocks for an entire week, what a joy it is to appear in Sunday School in such an airy, exquisite trifle as this little batiste model.

The skirt, which is of straight pieces made very interesting by a group of pin tucks edged with insertion, joins a waist portion that depends on the shaping of its lower edge and a few delicate sprays of embroidery for its individuality.

Val lace trims all the edges of the dress and the loveliest of pink ribbon sash ends extended from the front tie in the back.

A little six-year-old miss would require about 2 yards of material 36 or 40 inches wide, from 8 to 9 yards of Val edging, 3 yards of insertion, and 2½ yards of ribbon.

Model 13D.—For a dark-haired and dark-eyed lassie who has already learned the lesson that often smartness and simplicity walk hand in hand, this pink ratiné model is recommended.

Outlining the shoulder seam and the neck and sleeve edges are three rows of wool darning-stitches, black, fuchsia, and green in color. These same colors are repeated in the battlement outline on the skirt and, in addition, colored wool pompons with stems of black fill each inverted battlement section.

For the average girl of eight, provide about 2 yards of 36-inch material and 6 or 7 small skeins of yarn.

Model 13E.—Who can help but become sturdy and robust when supplied with play frocks such as this, which fairly urge one into the open and then incite the most active of sports?

Of taffy-colored chambray, this model is one that is practical in every detail. The skirt portion is cut separate from the waist and has considerable fulness held by several rows of black smocking, which forms a shallow yoke effect. The collar and vestee are of white Indian head.

Below the vest, the waist closing, emphasized by bound buttonholes and self-covered buttons, is effected by means of a fly portion. Then the waist and skirt are finished separately from the center front to the skirt placket at the left side.

Made with bloomers, this little frock requires 3 or 3¼ yards of 36-inch material, ⅛ yard of contrasting color, and 2 or 3 skeins of floss for the average child of six.

Model 13F.—Green-and-white linen, appliqué in several harmonizing colors, and black ciré ribbon are combined with admirable results and to mutual advantage in this very distinctive one-piece model.

The sash, by extending under the waist line at the center front, detracts in no way from the odd cut and the appliqué, and provides a novel arrangement that is a relief from the usual encircling effect. Bindings of white finish the front edges of the dress and the outer edges of the collar and cuffs.

As a rule, 2¼ yards of material and 2¾ yards of narrow ribbon are sufficient for an eight-year-old girl.

Novelty Apparent in Children's Shoes

Aside from the stubby oxfords and high shoes of staple variety, which, because of their comfort-giving qualities and very practical nature, will undoubtedly never wane in popularity, novelty is apparent in both the detail and the color of children's shoes.

Patterned after big sister's very best pumps are miniature single- or double-strapped patent-leather slippers, some entirely in black, others with the gray back, which sister values so highly for their smartness. And then there are sports models, replicas as to color combinations of grown-up styles.

It is in the tiny Russian boots that the wee maiden finds a distinction from the mature influence. These are usually of black or brown calf, some of the black models having red trimming, but are particularly fascinating when they are made of black patent leather and cuffed in white.

 ©2016 Amy Barickman, LLC

Model 13

13 C

13 A

13 B

13 D

13 E

13 F

Tiny-Tot Styles

Model 14.—One thing the back and front of this little model agreed to was that the skirt portion should have considerable fulness. But when it came to the manner of adding fulness by means of full-length box plaits stitched underneath from neck to waist line, the back took the very practical stand that its box plaits would require pressing too frequently and insisted that its fulness be gathered into a yoke portion and be restrained somewhat by a narrow belt.

Blue chambray for the dress, fine-ribbed white piqué for the collar and cuffs, and fine white rickrack braid for edging a portion of the box plaits make up the dress as shown.

As the neck line is rather close, it would not permit the dress to be slipped over the head without another opening, and so this is made at the center back, which requires that the neck edge of the left side of the dress and of the collar be left open from the center front to the center back.

For a little girl of four, 1¾ yards of 32- or 36-inch material, ¼ yard of contrasting color, and about ¾ yard of rickrack are required.

Model 14A.—There is a great advantage in being able to count one's years on the fingers of one hand when this possibility includes such privileges as the wearing of frocks of this type.

Pink-and-white printed cotton is the material of which it is fashioned, white organdie the fabric of which the frills are made, and smocking and lazy-daisy-stitches in pink the trimming that decorates each side front. An enlarged detail of the embroidery is shown at the right.

The opening at the center front is finished with a white binding and supplied with loops and organdie buttons.

Provide for a child of four about 1¾ yards of material for the dress. For the collar and cuff plaitings, supply ⅜ yard of material or ⅞ to 1 yard of frilling. The embroidery requires about 2 skeins of floss.

Model 14B.—A slavish following of Fashion's whims and fancies may be all right for girls who are not concerned with the more important things of life, but not for the small boy whose time is filled to the limit with the most engaging of pursuits. Little he cares whether Fashion is favoring high or low waist lines, or plain or gathered sleeves, as long as he is supplied with comfortable, sturdy suits of this type, which do not hamper his activities in any way.

Green romper cloth is the fabric employed, and white cotton poplin, the material of which the collar, cuffs, and belt are made. Although the design is not unusual, the belt, by a series of interlacings through faced slashes, gives the suit an individuality that is very pleasing.

The front closing is emphasized by an applied strip of material pointed at the lower end. The pocket, although not conspicuous, is the very nicest part of the suit—that is, in the small boy's estimation. And anyway, what boy's suit could ever be considered complete unless supplied with pockets?

For a little lad of four years, 2¼ yards of material 36 inches wide and ⅜ yard of contrasting color are required for this suit.

Model 14C.—Just as much serviceability and truly as much freedom as could be desired in any suit may be found in this model of brown-and-tan chambray. But these aren't the only points in its favor, for its waist and trousers are made separately—quite a departure from rompers, to be sure!

An average child of three years requires 2 yards of material 32 inches wide for a design such as this. About ⅜ yard of contrasting fabric is needed for the collar and cuffs.

In cutting out the waist of the little suit, make it extend about 2 inches below the waist line. Then, in making it, provide a

stay piece for the buttons by adjusting the waist-line fulness under a straight strip of material cut the same length as the measurement of the waist line of the trousers. After the fulness is adjusted, secure the stay strip by turning under both edges and stitching them flat to the waist.

Either face or hem the upper edge of the trouser portion, and supply this with buttonholes placed at comparatively close intervals. Then secure buttons to the waist.

Model 14D.—When mother is planning a suit for one's very best, what is there to do but let her pent-up desire for frills and fussings find just a small outlet, provided, of course, that she uses these frills in a manner entirely becoming to manly attire? Certainly there is nothing girlish about this little suit of blue and white linen, and yet it relies as much on trimming as does many a wee maiden's dress. But these trimmings are applied in such a sensible manner—mostly as bindings to accentuate the details of the design, and in just sufficient frilling to draw attention to the smart collar and vest.

For an average tot of three years, provide 1½ yards of material with ½ yard of contrasting color for collar, vest, frills, and bindings.

Cotton poplin might be used to excellent advantage in a suit of this style, and white lawn or dimity selected for the trimming.

Model 14E.—All the niceties of peasant influence are combined with strictly modern conceptions of what is desirable in children's frocks for this delightful little model of white crêpe de Chine. The trimming, which is applied in such an interesting manner, is of cross-stitch embroidery in harmonizing hues of violet, red, and green.

The tiny fitted yoke, so shallow that one would hardly identify it, is made double and finished on both edges with short blanket-stitches worked in red. The dress fulness is constrained by several close rows of shirring and the raw edge concealed between the two yoke thicknesses. At the center front, the dress is slashed to permit of its being slipped over the head easily. The slash is finished with a facing, and the edges are held together at the neck line with a cord of red silk that matches the embroidery floss. The raglan sleeves are simply finished with a very narrow band of self-material, which confines the sleeve fulness and permits a frilled effect.

Fine white voile would be a very good selection for a little dress of this style. Of this or any material 36 or 40 inches wide, 1¾ yards will be needed for the average child of four.

Model 14F.—Even though spring has arrived with promises of balmy days and the wispiest of summer frocks with which to enjoy them, it is well to remember that she has ever been known to be fickle and is apt to revert suddenly to chill, rasping winds that make one long for the comfort of a warm, sheltering coat.

For just such occasions, this very practical tweed model is suggested. Surely, it is not wintry in appearance, for it is of a lovely green-and-rose mixture, but, withal, it provides ample protection against spring's caprices or the occasional chill of a summer evening. An armhole dropped several inches below its normal position and blanket-stitched with green yarn in the most engaging manner, is the unusual feature of the design.

This is just one of the many lovely tweed models that Fashion has planned for children and juniors. Bright blues, soft rose, lavender, and the usual gray or brown mixtures are the dominant colors, while the cut is considerably more versatile but seldom intricate.

For the average child of four years, 1½ yards of material 54 inches wide, 1¾ yards of lining fabric, one small skein of yarn, and six molds for the self-covered buttons are required.

Model 14

14 a

14 B

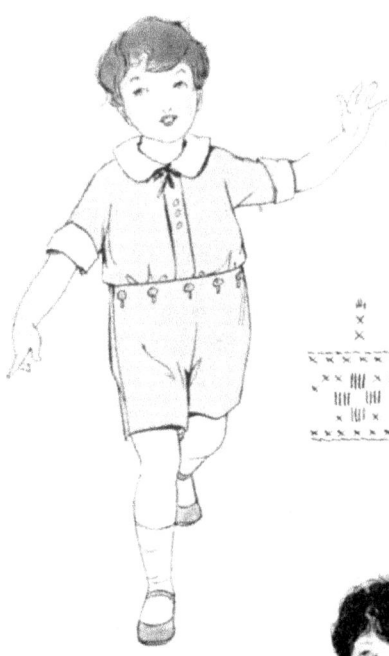

14 C

14 E

14 D

14 F

Magic Pattern: *Shoulder Bolero*

This is an original Magic Pattern, a project you cut out using diagrams instead of pattern pieces. These were first created by Mary Brooks Picken for the Woman's Institute's student magazines, *Inspiration* and *Fashion Service*. My book **Vintage Notions: An Inspirational Guide to Needlework, Cooking, Sewing, Fashion & Fun** featured 12 original Magic Patterns. Recently I have created modern patterns that were inspired by these vintage gems featured in the book **The Magic Pattern Book**, which I licensed with Workman Publishing. We have chosen to keep the authenticity of this original pattern intact and therefore have not changed instructions based on modern fabrics and techniques. Note at the end of this pattern you will find helpful tips for drafting pattern pieces.

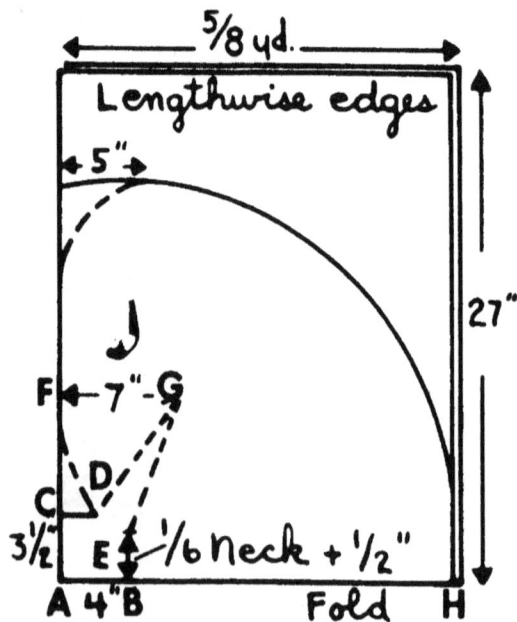

▶▶▶ MAKE THIS BOLERO of fake fur white krimmer, lined with jersey to match dress.

You need ⅝ yd. of 52- to 54-in. fake fur fabric and the same amount of tubular jersey for lining, plus thread, of course.

To chalk out: Fold fabric lengthwise, wrong side out. Pin edges together and lay fold toward you. Mark for cutting, following the diagram. Point *B* is 4 in. to right of corner *A*. *C* is 3½ in. above *A*. *D* is 1½ in. to right of *C*. *E* is one-sixth of the neck measurement plus ½ in. above *B*. *F* is 7 in. above *C*. *G* is 7 in. to right of *F*. Connect *D* and *E* with *G* to get shoulder dart, as dotted lines on diagram show. Tie a string to a pencil and, holding string at *E*, swing an arc from corner *H* to edge of fabric above *F*. Curve front line as dotted line shows; also curve from *F* to *D*. Cut on these dotted lines *D* to *F*, *F* around curve to *H*. Pin shoulder darts, pinning each dart in from *G*. Put cape on; pin edges together at underarm, and make sure that neckline is comfortable.

Remove. Open darts. Cut lining exactly same size. Pin darts in bolero and lining and baste and stitch these. Cut seams of darts open and press them open. Lay right sides of lining and bolero together. Stitch all around edge, leaving only neck unstitched. Press seam open and turn right side out. Trim raw edge of lining in at neck and whip it down to conceal seam. Put garment on, catch edges together to form bottom of sleeves. Whip these together, and your bolero is done and ready for wear.

Your Measurement Chart & Notes on Making Magic Patterns

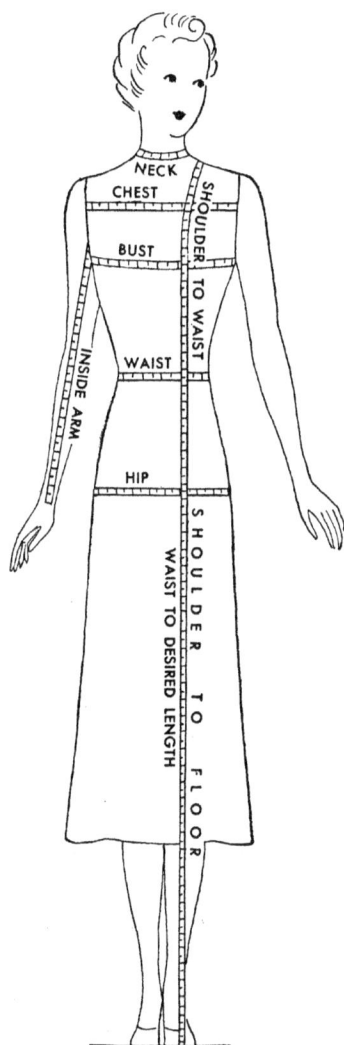

BUST (Fullest Part)............._____

WAIST ...._____

HIP (Fullest Part) ...._____

WIDTH OF CHEST..........._____

FRONT WAIST LENGTH
Shoulder to Waist............._____

FRONT SKIRT LENGTH
Waist to Desired Length........._____

FRONT FULL LENGTH
Shoulder to Floor ...._____

NECK (At Base) ...._____

SHOULDER
Neck to Armhole Line..........._____

ARMHOLE ...._____

WIDTH OF BACK ...._____

BACK LENGTH
Neck to Waist ...._____

BACK LENGTH
Neck to Floor..............._____

OUTSIDE ARM
Shoulder to Wrist (Arm Bent)...._____

INSIDE ARM
Armhole to Wrist (Arm Straight).._____

UPPER ARM (Fullest Part)......._____

ELBOW (Arm Bent) ...._____

WRIST ...._____

HAND (Closed) ...._____

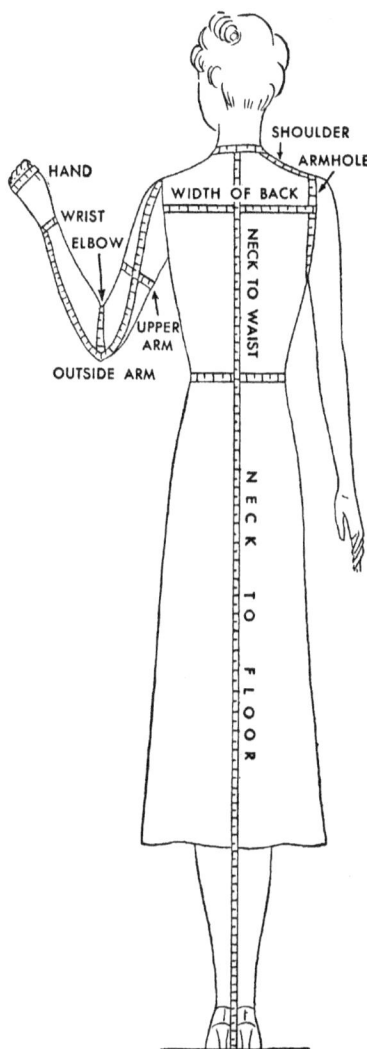

Keep Accurate Measurements

Since the garments in this book are all cut from measurements, it is necessary to have accurate ones to follow. Keep a list of your own measurements always at hand for ready reference.

Measurements for fitted garments should be taken over the type of foundation garments you expect to wear with them. Remove dress, jacket, or coat, which would distort the measurements. Do not take measurements too tight. Make all easy enough for comfort. The chart shows how to place the tape correctly for each measurement.

Making The Pattern

If you have the least doubt about your ability to chalk out the garment on your fabric, then rough it out first with crayon or heavy pencil on wrapping paper or newspaper. Cut out the paper pattern and use it to cut your garment. Cutting from a diagram, you can be sure that the proportions are correct for your size and that the garment will be a good fit.

How to Start Your Studies

Read This First

Woman's Institute
of Domestic Arts & Sciences, Inc.
Scranton, Pa.

As a collector of Woman's Institute content, I love finding original course work of students. The school published leaflets that were lessons as part of each course of study. The students corresponded mailing samples of sewing techniques as well as exams in to the school's instructors. I found this pamphlet explaining *"How to Start Your Studies"* and thought it was an interesting piece of information explaining the institute's processes.

Inside front cover.

Important Suggestions—

To help us give you our best service:

Place your *name* and *address* on all reports, letters, and envelopes that you send to us.

Write your *class letter and number* on all reports, letters, and envelopes that you send to us.

Fill in the *entire* heading at the top of each sheet of Answer Paper.

Always send a *complete* report and enclose your entire work in *one* envelope.

Send in *one* report at a time. Do not hold any report until you have completed a second one.

Although most women took the Institute studies as a correspondence course, lessons were also given at the school in Scranton.

Originally published in *How to Start Your Studies* booklet, 1923.

Woman's Institute Building, Scranton, Pa.

YOU are now a full-fledged member of the Woman's Institute, which means that you have at your service 450 people who are ready to help you realize from your investment with us the largest possible dividends.

We start with the mutual understanding that we are going to give to this undertaking the best that is in us, and with earnestness and determination on your part as well as on ours you can count on success for your work.

This little booklet will show you each step in the preparation of your reports. Keep it near you whenever you work on a report and follow the steps described here just as they come up.

Your Class Letter and Number

When your Application for Membership came to us, we immediately put your name and address

1

Originally published in *How to Start Your Studies* booklet, 1923.

on our records and assigned to you a *class letter and number* that are all your own. No other student should use them. They belong to you. They are for our convenience in keeping a complete record of your studies and correspondence. The number shows the order of your enrolment, and the class letter indicates which course or courses you are taking. Thus, by giving a class letter and number to each student and by each student *using* that class letter and number, we are able to keep accurate records. Every time you write your name on a letter, a report, or any other communication to us, *also give your class letter and number.*

You will naturally ask, "What are my class letter and number?" You will find them on your *Membership Card,* which we sent you by first-class mail with a letter from Mrs. Picken welcoming you as a student. On the face of the card are given your name, address, and class letter and number.

Please remember this. It is important.
Put your name, address, and class letter and number on every communication you send us.

Your Let's Get Acquainted Slip

With this same letter and card, Mrs. Picken also enclosed a slip headed "Let's Get Acquainted." Did you find it? If not, won't you look for it right now? It is very important that we become acquainted with you, so we devised this slip for this purpose. Answer every one of the questions asked on the slip. Then send the slip to us *immediately* so that we can begin to know you before your first report comes. The information you send us is

Originally published in *How to Start Your Studies* booklet, 1923.

carefully recorded. So, each time we receive a letter or a report from you, we can refer to our record of you and thus give you much better service than if we did not know you in this intimate way.

Regular Study Time and Place

A regular study *time* and a regular study *place* are two things that will help you progress rapidly with your studies.

It may be difficult for you to find a regular study time, but systematic study always brings better results than haphazard study. So, if possible, won't you set aside a certain time for study and then try to stick to it?

Also, arrange to keep all your study material together. A box, a drawer, a shelf, or some spot where everything with which you study can be kept and where you may return your Instruction Books and sewing when you are obliged to lay them aside will mean the saving of many, many minutes that may be put into study. Try, if you can, to have your study place located near your sewing machine for this will be a great convenience.

Studying Your Instruction Books

And now, with these preliminary steps taken care of, you are ready to

3

Article written by Mary Brooks Picken, May 1935

Arrange sheets in their proper order and pin them together HERE. Do not write questions on these sheets. Number each answer to correspond with the question, but do not write out the question. Only the answer is required.

Woman's Institute
of Domestic Arts & Sciences, Inc.
Scranton, Pa.

ANSWER SHEET FOR EXAMINATION QUESTIONS

Remember to write your full name and address, and class letters and number plainly on this sheet and on the envelopes so that there will be no loss of delays. Advise us promptly and definitely of any change of name or address.

Use both sides of this paper, as it saves postage for you and us. After filling this side, use the reverse side, beginning at the other end.

Sheet No. *1*

Name of Instruction Book *Essential Stitches and Seams* Part No. *401*

Your Name *Mrs. Jane Sampson* Class Letters and Number *D.F. 000000*

Street and Number] Box, or R. F. D. No.} *1600 Wyoming Ave.,* Post Office *Scranton* State or] Country} *Pa.*

PRINTED IN U.S.A.   6WI

1. Needles, pins, thimble, scissors or shears, tracing wheel, ripping knife, and tape line.

2. To purchase one with sharp, even points.

3. To determine whether the tension is properly adjusted.

4 (a). All parts designated on the machine, and all parts that rub together.

4 (b). When in constant use, oil every day; but if not used so often, once a week is sufficient.

5. By overcasting, notching, or binding.

Originally published in *How to Start Your Studies* booklet, 1923.

begin the study of the first Instruction Book, which is *Essential Stitches and Seams.* **First read this Book from beginning to end** and try to understand each point as you proceed with the reading. If you come to some point that does not seem entirely clear to you, do not be discouraged, but **mark the part with lead pencil and go back to it again when your mind is refreshed.** When you are obliged to lay your Instruction Book aside, mark your place so that you will waste no time in looking for it when you take it up again. If, after conscientious study, there are points still not clear, write to us, using the "Information Blanks" sent you for this purpose.

Preparing Your Reports

When you have read and studied your Instruction Book until you feel that you know just what is meant by every part of it and have practiced the various stitches and seams, you are ready to make out your first report.

Now let us help you get this report ready to send to us. To enable us to take care of your work promptly, we need to have:

> **Your full name, clearly written**
> **Your complete address**
> **Your class letter and number**

On the opposite page is shown a sample of the first page of a student's report. Look this over very carefully so that you may know just how we wish you

4

Originally published in *How to Start Your Studies* booklet, 1923.

to prepare your reports. Then fill in the heading and write out your answers, leaving spaces between them, as shown, and using both sides of the paper.

With your answers you are to send to us the apron, made according to the instructions you have received, and the four samplers that are required.

Mailing Your Work

You will find that we have provided a special envelope to carry all this to us, and in the illustration on this page you learn just how to use it. First,

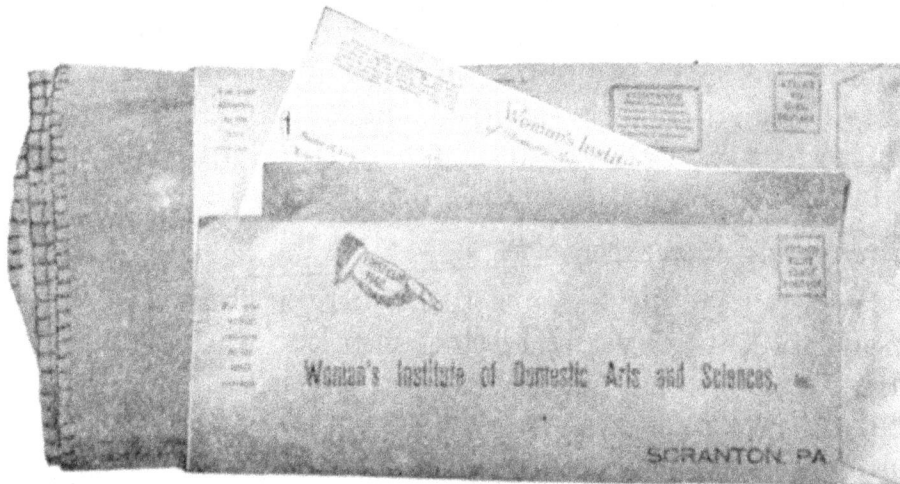

put your folded report in the pocket-like part on the front of the envelope. If there is just one sheet, as there probably will be, put a two-cent stamp on this part of the envelope and seal the flap down tight. (This written work must come as first-class mail, a two-cent stamp carrying four sheets.)

Now lay your samplers inside of your apron and fold this to fit into the large part of the envelope.

6

Originally published in *How to Start Your Studies* booklet, 1923.

Seal this part also, and have your postmaster weigh it for you, putting on the amount of postage that is required for parcel-post rates.

Send this to us, and while you are waiting for its return, go on with the study of your next Instruction book, *Simplified Sewing*.

Remember that we are here to help you, so write to us when you need help. If we work together toward the goal we have set, it will not be long before you will be realizing many benefits from your studies.

These Questions and Answers May Save Time for You. Read Them Thoughtfully

1. You have explained how I should send my report on *Essential Stitches and Seams*, but how should I send *Simplified Sewing* and similar reports that do not require the making of garments?

Ans. Send your written answers and samplers on *Simplified Sewing* together. Put them in one of the

7

Originally published in *How to Start Your Studies* booklet, 1923.

regular return envelopes, 4 inches $\times$ 9$\frac{1}{2}$ inches, sent you for this purpose, and send them as "First-Class Mail." Follow this plan with all reports except *Dress Development*, with which you should send the home dress, using the special large envelope in the same way that you were instructed to use it for *Essential Stitches and Seams*.

2. Should I prepare and send several reports at one time?

Ans. No. Prepare all the work required **for** **one** report and send it as soon as completed. Then work on the next report while you are waiting for the other to be returned.

3. How long is it before you return my corrected report?

Ans. This depends on how far you live from Scranton and on how much congestion there may be in the mails. We try to return reports within 3 or 4 days after they reach us. But in an unusual rush of work it is not possible for us to do this. Delays are apt to result unless you observe the following:

Always give your class letter and number.
Sign your full name and your address.
Sign your name always in the same way and as it is shown on your Membership Card.
Put sufficient postage on the envelope.
Put all of your report in **one** envelope.
Notify us of a change of address.

Originally published in *How to Start Your Studies* booklet, 1923.

Final Suggestions—

Study at least a little *every* day.

Plan *special* days when you can devote considerable time to study.

Put into *practice* as quickly as possible the various principles you learn in order that they may be yours for all time.

Read over your written lesson reports before sending them to us, not only to make sure that they are *complete*, but to derive benefit from the *review*.

Put your *class letter and number* on everything you send us, and also write your *name* and *address* clearly.

Woman's Institute
Scranton, Pa.

Originally published in *How to Start Your Studies* booklet, 1923.

Vintage Notions Monthly continues to share the work of Mary Brooks Picken and the Woman's Institute which inspired my book *Vintage Notions*. Although the Institute was founded 100 years ago, the treasure trove of lessons and stories are still relevant today and offer a blueprint for living a contented life.

If you enjoyed this issue of *Vintage Notions Monthly*, visit AmyBarickman.com for more of my curated collection of vintage content including patterns and books for needle and thread, inspiring fabric, textiles & free vintage art. Be sure to subscribe to my **Amy Barickman Studio YouTube Channel** where I share fascinating sewing and fashion history along with timeless style and DIY technique for your modern making!

www.amybarickman.com
Subscribe to my eNewsletters
Follow my creative journey!
Learn about new products, videos, special offers, and receive a FREE PDF gift filled with
Vintage Made Modern printable and
a Cropped Jacket Magic Pattern.

Join my Community
Further your skills and enhance your knowledge with fellow vintage-inspired creative spirits!
Amy Barickman's Vintage Made Modern Facebook Group
Amy Barickman Studio YouTube Channel
Amy Barickman Studio Facebook Page
AmyBarickman Studio Instagram

Inspiration Vintage Notions Monthly, Volume 1, Issue 6 (VN0106)

All rights reserved. Printed in USA. No part of this publication covered by the copyrights herein may be used in any form of reproduced by any means—graphic, electronic, or mechanical, including photocopying, recording, except for excerpts in the context for reviews, without written permission of the publisher. Purchasing this book represents agreement that the buyer will use this book for personal use only, not for reproduction or resale in whole or in part. The original, rare content is in the public domain;however this restored and revised edition has been created from my personal collection and is protected by copyright.

To reach Amy email amyb@amybarickman.com

www.ingramcontent.com/pod-product-compliance
Lightning Source LLC
LaVergne TN
LVHW061330060426
835513LV00015B/1350